MINDFUL LEADERSHIP

7 steps to transforming
your business and your life

Michele Gennoe

Published in Australia by
The Women's Achievement Institute
PO Box 476, Neutral Bay, NSW 2089, Australia
ABN 64 503 612 989
www.twa.institute

All rights reserved. The moral right of the author has been asserted.
No part of this book may be reproduced by any person or entity, including internet search engines or retailers, in any form or by any means, electronic or mechanical, including photocopying (except under the statutory exceptions provisions of the Australian Copyright Act 1968), recording, scanning or by any information storage retrieval system without the prior written permission of the publisher.

National Library of Australia Cataloguing-in-Publication entry

A catalogue record for this book is available from the National Library of Australia

Author: Gennoe, Michele, author.
Title: Mindful Leadership : 7 steps to transforming your business and your life / Michele Gennoe

ISBN: 978-0-9925998-1-2 (paperback)
ISBN: 978-0-9925998-2-9 (ebook)

Subjects: Leadership, success in business, work-life balance

Dewey Number: 158.4

Disclaimer: Any opinions expressed in this work are exclusively those of the author and are not necessarily the views held or endorsed by others quoted throughout. All the information, exercises and concepts contained within this publication are intended for general information only. The author does not take any responsibility for any choices that any individual or organisation may make with this information in the business, personal, financial, familial, or other areas of life based on the choice to use this information. If any individual or organisation does wish to implement the steps discussed herein it is recommended that they obtain their own independent advice specific for their circumstances.

Editor: Sumitra Menon
Layout design: Verve Design
Cover design: Sophie White Design
Model designs: Maria Revenko

Printed by Ingram Spark

This book is available online at www.michelegennoe.com, Amazon and other online bookstores.

Copyright © 2014 Michele Gennoe
All rights reserved
First Published in Australia 2014
ISBN: 978-0-9925998-0-5

*This book is dedicated to the village elders
who helped to create this experience
and to the change makers who, regardless of race,
creed, colour, situation or circumstances,
are actively creating a world where
love is the only currency,
joy is the everyday fashion and
humanity lives in the blessings of each moment...*

CONTENTS

Foreword vii

Part One: *The Journey Begins*
Chapter 1: Introduction 03
Chapter 2: A New Paradigm for Corporate Thinking 13

Part Two: *The 7 Steps to being a Mindful Leader*
Chapter 3: I think therefore I have Purpose 23
Chapter 4: Fearlessly letting Passion create your daily calendar . . 33
Chapter 5: Pathways to intuitive decision-making 47
Chapter 6: Valuing the People and relationships in your life 59
Chapter 7: Giving creates Prosperity and makes you handsome . . 69
Chapter 8: Being mindful to the Pausing moments between
each breath 81
Chapter 9: Presence is being dressed from within 97

Part Three: *Where to from here?*
Chapter 10: Conclusion 111
Appendix: Selected exercises 119

Bibliography 149
Acknowledgements 151
Further Information 153

FOREWORD

Mindfulness and the notion of Mindful Leadership are big concepts and ones that leaders are embracing more and more as part of the formulae for business success in the digital era. In the same way the world changed with the industrial revolution, the digital age has brought a range of new paradigms of thinking to society.

As our day to day worlds are changing, so too the worlds of work and business are experiencing enormous change. As organisations downsize and working at home becomes more and more prevalent, mindful leadership becomes not just about instructing people what to do, but instinctively empowering them to excel in the pursuit of a shared vision.

As a businesswoman and change maker within my own industry, I first met Michele Gennoe at a gathering of like-minded people where she was volunteering as CEO for the organisation. Michele was sharing her unique perspectives, discussed throughout this book, whilst also doing voluntary work for the organisation (a core component of her approach to business).

Now Michele offers you what once only million dollar corporations could afford - the insights of a high level change maker, in her book *"Mindful Leadership: 7 steps to transforming your business and your life"*. It's both a framework for her unique approach and an easy-to-follow program that will guide and inspire. If you're feeling lost in the constant change of the 21st century, I highly recommend that you read each of these chapters with an open mind, an open heart, driven by the joy of discovery.

The insights you learn through Michele's processes will not only show you many great aspects of your leadership style but also what drives your personal levels of happiness and satisfaction.

Any manager who wishes to lead, or leaders who want to be the best version of themselves, can now take their businesses and their lives to greater depths and levels through these insights. Most importantly they will be able to truly connect with who they are as a person, beyond their roles, and more meaningfully enjoy their lives.

I also believe that understanding our leadership strengths is key to living our greatest adventure. But great leadership is a skillset rather than a title. It's about taking the initiative to evolve, invigorate, inspire and lead by example. I also believe that as our working and personal lives become more and more integrated, it's important that we all become leaders. It's not all down to the people in head office any more, great leadership is about a skillset rather than a title. It's about taking the initiative to improve all areas of your life, it's what people once called "leading by example". Great and mindful leadership is for me, about being the best you can be, whoever you are and whatever you may be doing in your life.

You've already made the most important first step by choosing *"Mindful Leadership: 7 steps to transforming your business and your life"*. By joining the call for more Mindful Leaders you become part of this important change for society and the planet! In years to come, this book will be acknowledged for the new frameworks it presented, the lives it touched and the systems it changed forever.

Danielle Lehrer
Founder, Forex Nation

PART ONE

THE JOURNEY BEGINS

- Introduction
- A New Paradigm for Corporate Thinking

INTRODUCTION

"The most important question to ask on the job is not 'What am I getting?'. The most important question to ask is 'What am I becoming?'" ~ Jim Rohn

When I led my first organisational transformation at the ripe young age of 20 I didn't even know to call it that. I thought we were just making the organisation more efficient and that was what you did as a leader. As Vice President of the Student Guild at my university I was in charge of student housing and as a business student, was ready to not just run the housing but then move on and run the world by the time I was 30. I truly believed, with the enthusiasm of youth, that everything was possible.

We moved the housing office, adjusted the staff responsibilities and improved processes, all with the idea that it would save money, make student interactions easier and create happier experiences for everyone. As a young enthusiastic leader I thought that I was creating a form of business utopia in transforming the housing office to this more efficient state. Very quickly though the students were unhappy because they couldn't find the office, staff were unsettled as they were now unsure of what their responsibilities were, and it took time for everyone to get used to the new improved processes. I returned to the university a few years after I had left. The housing office had moved once again back to where it had been when I first took charge of it, and I feel certain that after a few more years was moved again.

Nearly 30 years on when I sat down to write this book on mindful leadership I wondered what it was I had really learnt that I could share with leaders, that was so different to my experiences as a 20-year-old? What is different today in the organisational changes that I work on with business leaders? What was it that I learnt from these experiences and took with each new experience into my next role and next one after that?

Over the years as I have worked with organisations in many countries the people were different, cultures and environments were different, but each of them in some way reflected my first experience of moving the student housing office: upsetting staff, confusing students, and everyone needing to learn how to do things in new ways.

What had changed over these years was that I had also been studying personal-development and trained as a coach, facilitator and trainer, and completed a Masters in Spiritual Science. Through this training in mindfulness I was then able to more intuitively understand what was going on behind the outward struggles and issues for the leaders of the organisations I worked with. These mindfulness trainings and seminars also changed the dynamics of the interactions that I had with the people I worked with. I would walk into a new organisation and within days the staff would think that I had always been in that organisation and accept that I knew what I was talking about. They would be amazed at how quickly I seemed to understand them and their organisation and how quickly I became integrated with where they were on their transformation journey.

This intuitive familiarity also took me a while to get used to as I then learnt to trust and respect it and could see that there were no accidents. People come together to work on different things at different times in their lives, and each of these moments is a perfect gift of what you are there to learn and teach in that interaction. Whether it is dignity under pressure, surrendering to what is, or finding gratitude for what is going right when all else seems to be going wrong, each of these choices of approach came from my training in maintaining mindfulness in the moment.

So this is my gift to you, wherever you are on your mindfulness journey, to the 20-year-old wanting to change the world, or the 40-year-old wanting to change their life. My intention with this offering is to assist you with what I have learnt from all of the personal development courses I have done, whilst working with leaders in organisations going through change. I believe that these mindfulness insights will assist in training you to understand on all levels ~ physically, mentally, emotionally and spiritually ~ what is going on for yourself, your organisation and your wider community. That it will allow you to become not just better leaders but happier and more balanced members of your families and of society as a whole.

What is the mind?

There are many approaches to defining what the mind is, which makes being precise about the definition much more elusive and open to interpretation. One definition states that the mind is related to the physical brain and the nervous system. But even if the mind is connected to the brain, it would still not be a single physical part of the brain, but a set of electronic impulses that pass through it. Unlike an arm or a leg there is no one specific single component of the brain that can be categorised as the mind. Another definition states that the mind is separate and distinct from the physical body; in other words, that the mind is one thing and the body is another.

Both of these approaches to defining the mind also look at the relationship of the mind to emotions, consciousness and soul.

Many great philosophical, religious and scientific scholars have discussed the mind in this way, dating back to philosophers such as Aristotle and Descartes.

Most agree that the mind does allow a person to be aware of their world and to identify the many different stimuli (noises, sights, smells) in order to be able to satisfactorily organise them. The organising of these inputs depends on perceptions that come from individual experiences, memories and thought processes that create a structure for those inputs. Whether you view your mind as being a part of your body or not, the outputs from processing the perceptions of your mind determine how you respond to the world, express opinions about, and act in different situations. The act of being mindful then is to be more consciously aware of how you are receiving, organising and structuring those inputs and outputs in the moment.

Seven challenges of mindful leaders

The leader of a team may, but does not always have to, be the manager or supervisor of that team. This is because leadership is not always a product of position or authority but one achieved by inspiration, persuasion and connections. The person who leads has the ability to have people follow them and take guidance from them, to create a specific result. In organisations, leadership is very important as it defines the direction of the organisation and whether or not the staff will support this direction. Only by communicating, motivating, inspiring and engaging with those they lead, can the leader achieve organisational success.

Effective leadership requires a time commitment and a willingness to learn these core leadership skills. Through understanding these skills you can enlist the support of your staff to deliberately change cultures when necessary and to lead your organisation to growing successfully.

A recent article in the Australian Financial Review states that "Companies that encourage mindfulness – which can be trained through regular meditation practice – claim they see absenteeism falling, productivity rising and business improving."[1] As a result mindfulness training is being implemented by organisations in industries such as telecommunications, finance, FMCG, government and other sectors.

The models and information presented throughout the 7 Steps described in the pages to come, reflect not only the lessons learnt throughout my career but are also supplemented with interviews of outstanding mindful leaders of Australian industry. The challenges facing all leaders are surprisingly more similar than they are different. The Centre for Creative Leadership released a white paper[2] in 2014 which showed that leaders face relatively similar challenges, irrespective of their location. The research that the Center conducted in seven different countries found that "... the most significant challenges these leaders face are relatively similar across all seven locations".

In consolidating my experience, interviews with industry leaders and the research from The Centre for Creative Leadership I have summarised this information into the following seven challenges which mindful leaders face. With the 7 Steps to overcoming these challenges through being a mindful leader presented in Part Two.

The seven challenges facing a mindful leader are:

Challenge 1: **Inspiring others**
To be inspirational and assist staff in exploring and discovering meaning in the work they do.

The 7 challenges facing a mindful leader	The 7 Steps to overcoming these challenges
Inspiring others	Purpose
Managing change	Passion
Maintaining effectiveness	Pathways
Developing & leading people	People
Giving back	Prosperity
Managing stress	Pausing
Living as Brand Me	Presence

*Challenge 2: **Managing change***
To be able to understand and lead change by aligning what you are doing with why you are doing it.

*Challenge 3: **Maintaining effectiveness***
To support and encourage the development of specific skills in decision-making and strategic thinking for increased ongoing effectiveness.

*Challenge 4: **Developing and leading people***
Developing the cohesion and collaboration between your team members so that they then become role models for the rest of the organisation.

*Challenge 5: **Giving back***
Working out appropriate ways to give back, whether that is through your time, money or in-kind support from you and the organisation.

*Challenge 6: **Managing stress***
With 24/7 connectivity it is harder, but increasingly important, to find downtime from meetings, emails or paperwork to recharge. Mindful leadership requires balance to manage this stress.

Challenge 7: **Living as Brand Me**
To manage the politics of relationships whilst managing up, getting buy-in from others and maintaining your leadership brand.

The net result of these challenges is that you are left needing to learn more in less time and manage ever-increasing complexities along the way. What follows are 7 Steps for leaders in how to lead and transform in an entirely different way ~ a mindful way that will assist you in managing the complexities of today and minimising the effects of these challenges. These mindfulness steps are also the keys to understanding who you are as a complete person in all the roles you play: as a family leader, a community leader, and as a leader of your own life, with each role reflecting how mindful you are as a person.

As you read through the information presented and do the reflective exercises it will change who you are as a person, in all areas of your life. There is no real need for separation into different roles or compartments in people's lives any more. A change in one area of your life leads to changes in all areas of your life. Like ripples from a pebble thrown into a pond, the changes ripple through to the entire pond.

7 Steps to overcoming a mindful leaders challenges

The rest of Part One continues with a comprehensive review of changes to leadership in the context of a New Paradigm for Corporate Thinking. The new paradigm examines how leadership now requires both structured and intuitive thought. At the intersection of these two thought processes is what is called Mindfulness. The old styles of thinking are still evident in the continuous restructuring in some sectors of business which continue to believe that doing the same thing will somehow produce different results. This applies just as much in more intuition-based organisations that never seem to grow because they fail to implement any real structures to support their growth.

Then through Part Two the 7 Steps to being a mindful leader are outlined: Purpose, Passion, Pathways, People, Prosperity, Pausing and Presence. Mindfulness will become part of who you are, not just what you do. Today's leader is no longer a motivator but an inspirer; no longer a figurehead but a part of the team; and no longer just a role, but a role-model.

There are many benefits of being a mindful leader, some of which can be quantified in terms of a return on investment (ROI) for the organisation. The ROI refers to the measurable quantification of success in terms of returns on money, time or resources, from putting a specific investment into an activity. In terms of money as an ROI, mindful leadership has led to increased rates of retention, employee satisfaction and overall engagement, which has then been shown to lead to an increase in productivity. Even more importantly, it has been shown to result in improved experiences for customers, which then flow onto the bottom line of increased sales.

In terms of time as an ROI, the time spent by staff in doing their day-to-day activities such as attending meetings and responding to emails, is made more productive with mindfulness. By having more focus in the moment, the staff then manage their diaries better, are more focused in meetings and prioritise emails more effectively. In terms of resources as a ROI, the energy levels of staff are increased when they have more awareness of their mind, body and state of being throughout the day. If staff take regular breaks, are eating well and doing some form of movement during the day, then their energy levels will stay up and this leads to increased productivity.

The operational resources are also then used in a more targeted and efficient manner due to the clarity and better focus of the staff using them.

Perhaps the most critical area of the return on investment in mindful leadership is that by doing some form of meditative practice, and becoming an observer of emotions, thoughts and feelings, you then start to observe your attachment to the ROI elements themselves. Becoming more aware of these attachments allows you to then detach from them. In this state of detachment you can then see more clearly whether your current focus of achieving goals, hitting targets and completing projects, is the right one in that moment for the organisation.

In developing this understanding of your emotional intelligence and your ability to identify, use, understand and manage emotions, you are better able to recognise your own emotional state and the emotional states of others. From this recognition, you are able to form better and healthier relationships with yourself and others. Identifying emotions also improves communication and empathy with others, which can really assist in times of conflict. A higher emotional intelligence can be used to improve relationships with people, have more success at work and lead a more rewarding and fulfilling life. In fact when it comes to having a happy and successful life, it has been suggested that emotional intelligence may be just as important as intellectual ability.

Part Three brings the 7 Steps together and provides selected exercises to further develop your mindfulness to add to your leadership toolkit and assist you with growing more as a successful mindful leader.

A NEW PARADIGM FOR CORPORATE THINKING

"We cannot solve our problems with the same thinking we used when we created them." ~ Albert Einstein

What is mindfulness?

Mindfulness is being aware of your thoughts, feelings, environment and bodily responses in each and every moment. It is being aware of each sensation or activity that is going on internally and externally, i.e. in your body as well as in your surroundings. Mindfulness brings your attention into the current moment, and by doing so allows you to then notice what is going on in and around you. Mindfulness can be applied to anything, in any area of your life, from walking to eating to leading meetings or writing emails.

Another part of mindfulness is that in the present moment whilst you are focusing you are also not judging anything that is observed but only noticing the thoughts, sounds, smells, etc. The key is to not become attached to what is observed but to just observe it. By remaining detached but curious about what is coming up in each moment it is also indirectly training you to accept what is present in that moment.

This training and acceptance in the moment is critical for you as it empowers you in your immediate choices. This is vital for a leader, whose decisions, attitude and behaviours lead to consequences that affect not only themselves but also the teams of people that they are leading.

The New Paradigm for Corporate Thinking presents mindfulness as the next step of traditional corporate thinking, and much more than a purely structured approach to managing in the moment.

What are structure and intuition?

The word "structure" as used in this book can also be defined as a framework. An organisational structure is a framework that defines roles and responsibilities - who does what, who reports to who, etc. - and provides a clear outline for them. Most, if not all, organisations have structures that are frameworks that by their nature define, delineate and delegate how each function, each ICT system, or HR system, etc. interacts with others. In this way the structure provides boundaries which determine how the organisation operates.

Intuition similarly has many different understandings or meanings, from gut reactions or instinct through to deja vu. For this book the definition is 'just knowing' in the way that people when they are driving their car may 'just know' that something is not right even if there is no obvious problem. The definition in this sense recognises that when you are mindful and in the moment you just know what to choose, decide, act on, etc. Parents have this with their children, a kind of sixth sense when something is not right, especially with babies. Teachers have similar experiences with kids in their class, as do good business leaders with their organisations. Sometimes things are not going right but the information you are receiving does not point to what the problem really is.

The New Paradigm for Corporate Thinking guides you to being more mindful in the moment by identifying whether the choices being made are from a structured (or habitual) pattern of thinking or from an intuitive (or gut) pattern of thinking. *Both are required for successful leadership today.*

CHAPTER 2: A NEW PARADIGM FOR CORPORATE THINKING

Model 1: A New Paradigm of Corporate Thinking

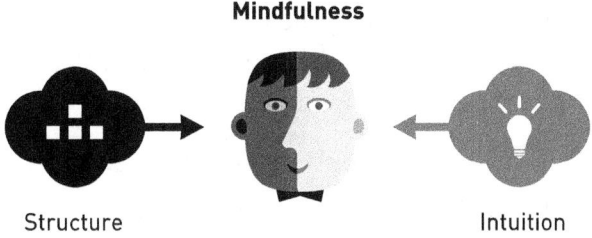

The habitual style of thinking made famous by Covey and others was a useful and appropriate approach to leadership before the world entered into the digital age. The pace of technology today means that leaders stuck in the habitual style of thinking will be left behind. Much like the old common belief that the world was flat and that you would fall off the end of it if you went too far, this type of fear keeps leaders stuck in a structured way of thinking.

Business schools have been very good at teaching us structure and providing instruction on how to build and lead structure in organisations. Personal development organisations have been very good at teaching us to connect to the self and to connect to our own inner guidance, our intuition. The digital age has created a wonderful time where both these different approaches are coming together under the banner of mindfulness.

There are also organisations that pride themselves on their organic style of leadership, which is very intuitive, and have resisted having structure, that cannot see either that the world is no longer flat. These organisations have resisted structure so as to remain fluid and flexible. But that same fluidity and flexibility stops them being able to grow. Some small business owners fall into this category as they just can't seem to let go of control by building more structure.

At the intersection of the structured and intuitive ways of thinking is mindfulness. What this means is that by taking the best elements of structure and the best elements of intuition and using these in a more mindful (aware) way, a leader can in each moment make the best decision for that moment.

There is a dynamic tension between structured and intuitive leadership that gives form to processes, lets go of form to allow for free intuitive thinking, or combines both. When determining how to lead people, processes and organisations, the balance of this dynamic lies in how to give it form (structured thought), while simultaneously leading from intuition (free thinking). There are no magic pills or answers that say that the correct response to situation X is action Y. With the speed at which things are changing now each situation and moment requires an individual mindful response.

Still restructuring and expecting different results?

Many organisations when going through a restructure, move the departments around, downsize or upsize. These actions are all based on the premise that if the structure and the staff related to what is being done are changed, then the organisation will be more efficient and profitable. Leaders identify where they are, where they want to be, and then manage the transition. This is the old paradigm of doing things over and over and expecting a different result. For some organisations this has also meant that the staff and culture have never reached any stability as their focus has always been on the next restructure.

The leading organisations of today have realised, however, that it is not about moving departments around, upsetting staff by firing many of their colleagues, or investing in the silver bullet consultancy 'solution'. Instead, they have invested, and keep investing, in their staff. With flat organisational structures, flexible roles, and by encouraging free-flowing creativity, these organisations have introduced a more mindful approach and begun to treat their staff as individuals and not just cogs in the organisational machine.

Organisations that still treat employees as cogs in the machine believe that with the advances in technology, staff should now be available 24/7 to respond to events, questions, and management's priorities, as a part of their job. Yet, if you were to question these same organisations about it working the other way, i.e. for time to be taken out of the 9-5 day for family situations, bills, and household management, there is not the same level of flexibility. In the digital age model with social connectedness, technology changing daily and globalisation at all levels, the role of a staff member has changed. More critically, just moving a staff member around from department to department as part of a restructure does not work either.

As a new paradigm leader, you are being asked to be more and more people-centric, and to do what you need to be more mindful (aware) of who you are as a person, of others in your spheres of influence and of world events. By understanding the complexity of your leadership role you can then empathise with those around you and place yourself in their shoes when need be.

Changing organisational and societal values

Organisations are not static and, like the rest of society, change and develop over time. What may have once been acceptable may be no longer acceptable. The roles of women, children and minorities have changed dramatically in the last 100 years in most developed countries and yet in other countries they may have changed very little at all. In a silver mine in Potosi, Bolivia, children still go down mines; women in some first world countries are still not allowed to drive a car on their own and minorities in many countries are still down-trodden.

What has changed and continues to change with both organisational and societal values, is the impact of the internet and instant access to information that this brings. The increased transparency of situations that may have been the norm in organisations and countries globally is now mobilising more people for change.

Working in organisations for the last thirty years over three continents has enabled me to see and contrast different sets of values which were the norms of the times in those organisations. Three examples below which stood out for me are presented not as good or bad examples, but to show the diversity of values in those organisations, and how what may have been acceptable or unacceptable in those times may now be called upon to change in this new socially connected world.

- The longest induction programme I ever completed was with a leading charity where all employees attended a week-long induction into the values of the organisation. By the end of the induction I understood what the organisation stood for, what my role was as an employee inside and outside of the organisation, the importance of the brand to the organisation and how the organisational values were inextricably linked to that brand. I had a very clear understanding that if I was an employee there than I was also signing up to those values and by the end of that induction week I had been engaged as a new custodian of the values that the charity stood for.

- In joining a leading bank, part of the induction process was an 'organisational fit' interview to match values after the standard preliminary technical interview stage. Once I had passed the 'organisational fit' interview I then proceeded to work in an environment of workplace bullying and harassment. This organisation had spent a lot of time and money trying to hire only people who matched their values, but once in, this exclusivity bred poor school-yard behaviours. Whilst there I learnt of a project that had run significantly over time and over budget and yet was celebrated as a big success because of the popularity of the manager, which again reinforced the school yard values that were a part of the 'organisational fit'.

- Whilst working at an educational institution I attended a staff meeting at which a senior manager told an employee who had been mugged the night before to 'toughen up and get over it'. He then went on to tell the male employees that using the on-campus security services indicated that they were not real men. This senior manager took pleasure in talking to me about taking tanks and running over parts of the campus that he did not like. Thankfully he was not typical of the staff in the university. However, the fact that he was not removed from his senior leadership role in spite of repeated reports to HR, spoke volumes of the values that this organisation held at this time.

Getting the cultural fit right for the staff that you want to have in your organisation is critical to not only your staff's experience of the organisation, but your clients, suppliers, vendors, and everyone else touched by your products and services. From school and by working in traditional organisations, leaders receive training and as a result can excel in how to think in a structured way. But it is through training in some form of personal development that leaders are able to develop their intuitive sides.

In Part Two the 7 Steps to being a mindful leader builds on the New Paradigm for Corporate Thinking and the dynamic tension between structure and intuition through specific steps. These steps are Purpose, Passion, Pathways, People, Prosperity, Pausing and Presence. It is by learning these steps and applying them that you are able to embrace more of the connection to your life by being a mindful leader.

PART TWO

THE 7 STEPS TO BEING A MINDFUL LEADER

Purpose

• Passion

• Pathways

• People

• Prosperity

• Pausing

• Presence

I THINK THEREFORE I HAVE PURPOSE

Covered in this chapter:

• Definition of Purpose

• Why Purpose is important to know now

• The Living on Purpose Model

• Why Purpose is essential for Leaders

• Interview with Gordon Cairns
Chairperson Woolworths Limited

"Man's search for meaning is the primary motivation in his life and not a "secondary rationalization" of instinctual drives. This meaning is unique and specific in that it must and can be fulfilled by him alone; only then does it achieve a significance which will satisfy his own will to meaning." ~ Viktor E. Frankl

Victor Frankl wrote one of the most famous books on meaning called *"Man's Search for Meaning"*. As a survivor of Nazi concentration camps he observed that the differences between those who died and those who survived in the camps came down to the presence or absence of meaning in their lives. Frankl believed that a person who knew the 'why' for his existence would be able to bear almost any 'how'.

The definition of purpose for this book then is similar to how Frankl has described it, in that it is what gives meaning and answers the 'why' question in the life of a mindful leader. Not everyone has a big or grand purpose in life but everyone has a meaning to being alive at this point in time and in being in the situations that they find themselves in. Whatever this purpose, and whether it is known or not, it is then reflected in all the areas of that person's life. Their jobs, their friends and family and hobbies, are all reflective of the underlying purpose that they are here to fulfil.

People may even define their purpose based on those things in their lives that have helped them to grow and moulded who they are as a person. For some there is a deep spiritual conviction in their lives, to which their purpose is closely aligned. For others there is this same sense of purpose when it comes to their family, work or money, or to some other hobby or activities that they are involved in. Some famous people who became known for their purpose are:

CHAPTER 3: I THINK THEREFORE I HAVE PURPOSE

> *"We will put a computer in every home in every office across America."*
> ~ Bill Gates

> *"You must be the change you want to see in the world."*
> ~ Gandhi

> *"I have a dream that someday this nation will live up to its creed that all men are created equal."*
> ~ Martin Luther King Jr

There was no school subject called Purpose 101 at the end of which these famous leaders received what their life purpose was, all nicely laid out for them. They themselves grew in their understanding of what they were here to do through the events in their lives. The people, events and circumstances of their lives then created who they were and what they understood they were here to do as individuals to fulfil their purpose.

Roy Baumeister and Kathleen Vohs, two eminent Professors in this field, when discussing how people give meaning to their lives and that everyone has this need, have proposed that "The seemingly universal development of meaningful interpretation also suggests that human beings are hardwired to seek meaning."[3] They suggest that there are four main needs for meaning of which the first is the need for purpose, "The essence of this need is that present events draw meaning from their connection with future events. The future events lend direction so that the present is seen as leading toward those eventual purposes."[4]

There has never been a more important time to connect with your purpose to give direction to the present. Humanity is going through exponential growth and change which is giving unprecedented options and choices to be, do and have anything that you want. So if you can have anything that you want, the question that then comes up is what is it that you really want to have or do and, who do you really want to be?

Why know your purpose now?

There are many examples of people reaching the top of their profession and then deciding that it wasn't actually what they wanted to do. Once they had reached that goal they sometimes changed direction for one of two reasons. Either they realised that they had changed on the journey and that the goal was no longer relevant or that they had been moving towards someone else's goals and that this was never what they wanted to do for themselves. So although they had achieved all that they had set out to do, the outcome then held no meaning for them.

There are times in life that can form a type of catalyst for change whether it is deliberately chosen or not. Some of these main catalysts are death, divorce and mid-life crisis.

People close to someone who has died, after the initial grief and shock has settled down, start to feel that there is something missing in their lives, that they are wasting time and need to do something now or it will be too late. There is a sense of urgency born out of this reminder of mortality that acts as a strong motivator for people to do something, change something.

Experiences following a divorce may be similar to those following the death of a loved one. In this case it is the death of the relationship that was built. As the roles and expectations for the new life after a divorce start to evolve and open up, people start to question what type of life they want to build for themselves. Now that there are different options, different choices that can be made, people open up to new possibilities, again with the same sense of urgency that time is short and things need to be done now.

This sense of urgency also comes forward in the period that has been described as "the mid-life crisis". By this stage people have usually reached a certain level of financial, relationship and career stability. But after all those years of working to reach that point, they may wake up one day and start to question if anything that they have is really what they want and if it is now too late to have the life that they recognise that they really wanted.

These major events in people's lives are times that in a sense force them to go outside of what is normal or usual for them. They are forced to go outside what is called their 'comfort zone' and to experience new changes.

The Living on Purpose Model

It doesn't always take a major event to be able to look at what your purpose is. There are every day and structured ways you can choose to go outside your comfort zone in order to connect with understanding your purpose. From simple acts like brushing your teeth with a different hand from the one that you usually use to brush them with, to sleeping on the other side of the bed from the side you are used to. The repetition of these simple acts of doing things differently can start to change the way you look at things, as they are moving you out of your everyday comfort zone.

Changing the way you look at simple everyday things can also show you where you are on the scale of being, doing and having in your life. Many people believe that if they have the right job and do well in that job then they will be happy. If this is turned around though and understood that the key is to focus on being, then no matter what you have or do, you are happy.

A significant part of the journey of that focus on being is in understanding what your purpose is in life. This gives people the meaning that they are looking for in their lives and empowers them to go out and be it.

Model 2. The Living on Purpose Model

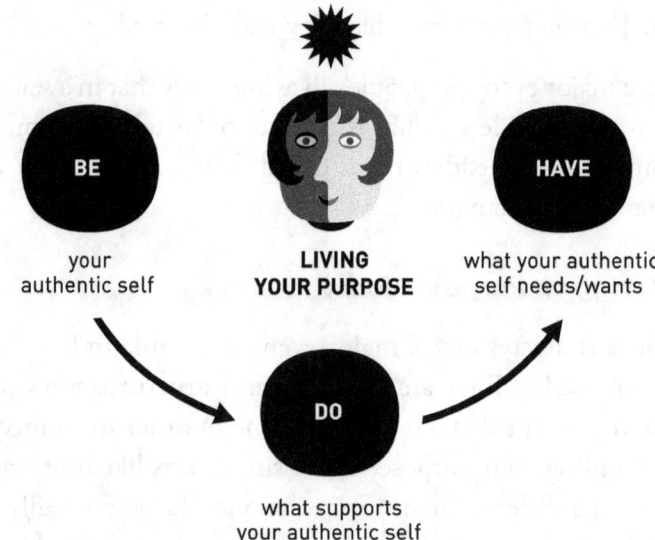

Why is purpose essential for leaders?

Self-belief and knowing who you are and what your purpose is in life is one of the most profound, empowering and valuable skills for any leader. It can serve as a compass through the good and difficult times in leading and is an essential leadership aspect of mindfulness. It gives meaning to life and purpose to the activities of life.

It is also imperative that if you as the leader have not set a direction to go in, and do not have an understanding of the purpose for this direction, then where are you by default leading yourself and others? Since nothing stands still, are you being led instead by situations, circumstances, or dominant personalities without being consciously aware of it? If you are being led by outside influences then how do you reconnect with where you want to go? The answer is that you do this by determining your purpose and then using this to set the direction for yourself and others that you lead.

Many leaders, however, may not feel able to take time out from their busy lives in the world. Being busy with what are essentially external activities, they are not aware of the need to attune to their own inner worlds. But find the time they must, in order to identify their purpose, and uncover the meaning that will become their cornerstone throughout all of their life.

Philosophers, religious leaders, poets, and many others have thought, discussed and even sung about people's purpose in life. All of them have at their core the concept of a personal connection to whatever higher power there is for them (God, Buddha, Allah, Spirit and others), and that they have an understanding of a larger purpose that they are alive for.

In the words of the now departed but not forgotten Steve Jobs:

"We don't get a chance to do that many things, and every one should be excellent. Because this is our life. Life is brief, and then you die, you know? And we've all chosen to do this with our lives. So it better be damn good. It better be worth it".[5]

MINDFUL LEADERSHIP

Interview: **The Sherpa Leader**

The first responsibility of a leader and of an organisation is to provide staff with meaning. In coming to work and giving up large amounts of their time and of their lives, people are trying to find meaning: why am I here? how should I act? who am I? Gordon believes that in explaining to staff as to why they have come together voluntarily to work in the organisation, and why the organisation exists, gives meaning to their being there.

Gordon sees it as the leader's role to provide the purpose behind the organisation, get collective agreement on the organisational values and then to authentically lead by walking the talk. By leading in this way people are treated like individuals and there is the power to change and transform people in a much larger way. In using results from a 360-degree feedback tool completed on himself, Gordon recognised that "the key learning for me was that fundamentally people are searching for meaning in their lives and the organisation is saying we will help you find it, we will help you transform yourself."

His mindfulness was triggered as he rose to the top of his profession when he realised that getting to the top of an organisation by just producing results is not enough because people will not follow you. By focusing on who you hire, fire and promote to support the type of organisation and the values you are promoting, you can transform the focus from being not just about results, to also being about how you have achieved those results.

In determining his own personal purpose Gordon walked the pilgrims Camino trail in Spain for 31 days in reflection and meditation. The lessons from that experience answered for him what his purpose was. "We are all climbing a mountain, and in climbing the mountain some of us struggle to carry our bags. That's my job

~ to carry their bags." With this purpose as a Sherpa to others, the opportunities to do this now finds Gordon metaphorically helping to carry other people's bags.

He sees that the role of the leader is to also help people to overcome their natural fear of looking at who they really are and in assisting them to want to transform themselves. The leader has to make it safe for them to do so, by providing feedback, programs and training to assist them with changing their behaviours, whilst supporting that there is nothing about the essence of people themselves that needs to be changed. Changing the behaviours at work also changes the behaviours in other areas of life as well, so that the benefits are felt in them being a better husband, better father and friend.

Gordon also uses meditation as a tool to calm his mind in business settings like preparing for meetings. In calming his mind he arrives at the meetings calm, centred and present. He is immediately present with where he is at in the moment and is not distracted by anything else, even when other people around him may be getting agitated by the same situation.

A compassionate man who is able to let go of the twists and turns on the road of his life, Gordon is always learning from what is present for him in each moment. In seeing that who you are is good, no matter what your behaviour, he is an inspirational leader of our time and a great example of a mindful man.

~ Gordon Cairns, Chairperson Woolworths Limited

Review: key lessons in the mindful leadership Purpose Step

- Your Purpose can reflect any area of your life
- Purpose is important to give meaning to your life
- In living on Purpose the focus is on being your authentic self, and you don't have to do or have anything for this
- Purpose is essential for Leaders to be able to lead others

To help integrate what has been covered in this chapter and to begin the journey of understanding Purpose more in your life, consider the questions below.

Reflective questions

1. What is it about your job, family, friends, hobbies that reflects you?
   _____
   _____

2. What are three of the most significant things to happen in your life?
   _____
   _____

3. If a significant event was to happen in your life tomorrow (death, divorce, crisis of meaning) what would you choose to do for the rest of your life?
   _____
   _____

4. What is stopping you doing what you answered in 3?
   _____
   _____

5. What is your purpose?
   _____
   _____

FEARLESSLY LETTING PASSION CREATE YOUR DAILY CALENDAR

Covered in this chapter:

• Definition of Passion

• Why Passion is Important to know now

• The Living your Passion Model

• Why Passion is essential for Leaders to manage change

• Interview with Ben Faiz, Managing Director Advanced ECO Solutions Pty Ltd

> *"If today were the last day of your life,*
> *would you want to do what you are about to do today?"*
> ~ Steve Jobs

Passion is at the very heart of what drives you to get out of bed in the morning and do what you do. It is the energy that fuels inspiration and is the enthusiasm and excitement for life. It enables you to keep going and to overcome obstacles because you just know that this is what you are meant to be doing. If knowing your purpose is about having meaning in your life, then passion is about doing the things that are in alignment with that.

Passion as defined in this sense is not an extreme, compelling or intense emotional driver. It is the emotional energy behind what inspires you to follow a pursuit. It is also not about letting what you are doing define who you are or why you are doing it. This distinction about passion is similar to the difference between living to work and working to live.

Living-to-work people can become workaholics who allow the obsessive nature of their passion to overwhelm them in all other areas of their lives. By letting the work define who they are, they have then become the work and not much else as a person. Yet many times people are not even aware that this is what they are doing, as workaholism, like other obsessive behaviour, often arises out of unconscious programming or other influences from their youth.

Why understand your passion now?

To live a life fully and mindfully you need to be aware of whose life it is that you are actually living. Is it the life that your parents outlined for you, that your family responsibilities have carved out

CHAPTER 4: FEARLESSLY LETTING PASSION CREATE YOUR DAILY CALENDAR

for you, or are you metaphorically in the driver's seat of the car of your own life?

Are the feelings that you are feeling or the thoughts that you are thinking yours and do they match what you are doing? Or are there times when there is a thought but no real feeling, or a feeling with no real thought and where do either the thoughts or feelings come from?

A good way of understanding how your background has influenced your thoughts and feelings is by reflecting what happens when people travel and expand their level of awareness from interacting with other cultures. For example, many cultures that outwardly are very poor are often rich in family and community values. Many first world people when they initially encounter this begin to recognise that it isn't always the possession of financial wealth that makes for rich lives and relationships, and that sometimes there are other elements to creating that in life.

From these experiences of travel your definition of 'richness' of life expands to include more than purely physical things. This increased awareness can lead to understanding that the family, culture, life that you were leading (and that had formed your habits up until that point) were not necessarily the only way to live.

Travel or some other form of expansion to your awareness allows you to become clearer about what you value in life and what you are passionate about. For business people this training in their passion also comes through the evolvement of their integrity in what they do.

The Living your Passion Model

From understanding what your purpose is in life and how you

reflect this in the world, you can then choose to live with passion, rather than having your passion running you. The living your passion model shows how, in aligning what you do for yourself, for others and for whatever you define as your higher power, you are aligning your activities to your overall meaning in life. It is important to note, however, that these activities in themselves do not provide the meaning.

Model 3. The Living your Passion Model

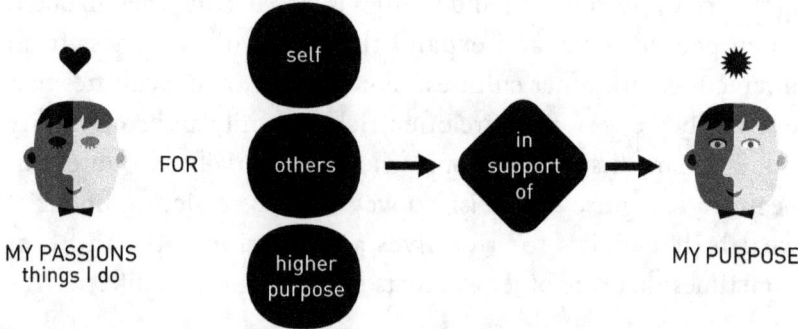

Why is understanding your passion essential for leaders?

Business ethics has mostly been seen by people as an oxymoron and political ethics as non-existent. Yet these business leaders and politicians put on their underwear one leg at a time in the morning like everyone else and it is very unlikely that they wake up in the morning and ask themselves "what unethical act can I do today?" So how do people's moral compasses go so far astray?

Your moral compass is your responsibility as it determines so much in the external world. With that responsibility there is also the opportunity to refine how it works for you. The Living with Passion Model can be used to view yourself holistically, as:

CHAPTER 4: FEARLESSLY LETTING PASSION CREATE YOUR DAILY CALENDAR

- an Individual (to self)
- a Business Leader (to others in the organisation and community)
- an innovative and inspiring Thought Leader (the world)

As an Individual (to self)

A lot has been written about the GFC around the globe and the unethical behaviours of those involved. Yet what those people were doing at the time would have been mostly normal business practices. If the enquiries, royal commissions and public debates have shown one thing over and over again, it is that the business leaders in these situations did not have a moral compass that pointed to their actions as being wrong or immoral. They saw it as being current business practice and that (even if it was on the edge of it) they were within their idea of the law at the time.

This is why the new paradigm and call to arms for being a leader requires you to lead from outside of current business practices, from outside of current ethical thinking, and attune to your own deeper level of integrity. You need to identify what is ethical to you and lines up with your values, regardless of what is happening around you.

- When working in London for a global media organisation I was tasked with organising the farewell for a senior vice president. The event went well but when it came to the bill for the function there were a number of contradictory discussions about it. Soon it became apparent that another senior executive had added the costs of the function to their business expenses without obtaining authorisation to do so. I flagged that these costs had appeared on these expenses knowing that it was

> likely I would be fired and I was. In this situation, the person himself had said that he would pay, the business had offered to pay and then they had colluded to try and hide the payment by submitting it through a different expense account. Other people in a similar situation may have chosen to collude with the 'current business practices' but I could not condone their actions as it went against my own personal integrity around transparency of actions.

You need to live with your own levels of integrity and respond to the world with your own moral compass. The key here for today and for now, is that in determining what your own moral compass is, you need to live and act on it, so that if challenged about something at a later date you are still congruent with why you took the actions that you took.

As a Business Leader (to others)

There are a number of ways to evaluate how others see you in the world, how you are interacting with that world, and the level of integrity that you are living by. Some of these are:

- 360-degree surveys. The 360-degree survey may or may not be activity based but it will give insights into how managers, peers and subordinates all see you on a range of skillsets and will point out areas for development in a very useful framework. Using Survey Monkey or a similar tool to conduct a survey can also provide anonymous feedback and insights around people's experiences of working with you.

- Running for positions. Nothing gives more direct feedback then placing yourself forward for a position and then asking for people's support. Putting yourself out there periodically and requesting support through votes, is a very direct feedback mechanism of what people are thinking of you.

- Level of reporting. As a business leader there is always reporting either up or down about the activities within the organisation and it often requires a very delicate balancing act. Reporting too openly and honestly about issues could be seen as bad management, and not reporting honestly enough as fraudulent activity. By providing a safe environment for accurate and authentic reporting, genuine information can be obtained and used as a feedback mechanism.

Each of these examples of identifying how others see you and see your actions in the world can provide good information about how your actions and behaviours are perceived. This then provides the information required to be able to take action and change and improve them.

The American Ethics Resource Center conducts national business ethics surveys which have tracked patterns and trends in the American workplace since 1994. The results from these surveys have shown that emphasising the importance of an ethical culture in organisations leads to an increase in the level of trust and a decrease in the risks in that business. The study in 2009 indicated "that strong ethical culture in a company has a profound impact on the kinds of workplace behaviour that can put a business in jeopardy."[6]

Australia is a big sporting nation and the topic of behaviours comes up often when the latest sports star has behaved in a way that is perhaps not the best example to their sport or more importantly to children who see them as role models. Rugby Union have an Integrity Office and Cricket Australia have recently created an

Integrity Unit and are posting advertisements for jobs like the one below. Whilst it is to be applauded that organisations like this are setting up internal controls the part in the advert which talks about an 'exciting, issues-rich environment' still raises for me questions around what may be common practices for these organisations and how embedded these issues are within these sports. It will be interesting to see whether integrity units will assist these sporting leaders to define what behaviours line up with living their purpose.

> - In this newly created role of Integrity Officer, you will work in an exciting, issues-rich environment as an important member of CA's recently established Integrity Unit. Reporting to the Senior Manager - Integrity, your key responsibilities will include a range of projects across each of the functional areas of the CA Integrity Unit, including CA's anti-doping and anti-corruption programs and the establishment and management of systems and processes that will help deliver the operational plan of the Unit. You will also be responsible for the gathering and analysis of relevant data and manage CA's relationships with betting operators. Your efforts will contribute to a greater accountability culture and an adherence to strong governance and risk management principles within Australian cricket.

As an innovative and inspiring Thought Leader (to the world)

In interviewing a number of business leaders for this book many of them saw in some way that they were not only leading from the front but they were there to serve their business, their community and their families in some way. This servant leadership energy is based on their understanding that there is a higher power at

CHAPTER 4: FEARLESSLY LETTING PASSION CREATE YOUR DAILY CALENDAR

work and that whatever their actions and activities, they as business leaders are leading individual people.

Knowing their personal purpose and the purpose of the organisation provides meaning to all. But what many leaders also identify is how their activities are helping others along the way and will ultimately be of benefit to all of humanity.

As the focal point and leader of change in the organisation, you are responsible for not only the structural elements of the change itself, but also for all the management of people in that change process. The challenge of managing people through this change, mobilising them to support it and overcoming their resistance to it, comes back to how authentically your ethical behaviours reflect the integrity of the change itself. You are also in a unique position to manage change for yourself, your organisation and for humanity as a whole.

With these opportunities comes the responsibility to not only do these things but to do them in a mindful way which supports those that are supporting you in the activities that you are leading. Famous leaders like Mandela and Gandhi are good examples of politicians who have profoundly impacted on those around them. After Gandhi's funeral General George C. Marshall, the American Secretary of State, said that:

> *"Mahatma Gandhi had become the spokesman for the conscience of mankind, a man who made humility and simple truth more powerful than empires."* [7]

Interview: **The Green Leader**

Ben had been working in a corporate job in the printing industry for many years. He had missed much of his children's lives for nearly 12 years and realised that he felt as if the organisation owned him. His turning point came when after leaving the office for the day he had to return to work for a meeting at 9.30pm only to be told that the whole point of that meeting was to set up another meeting a few days later.

Ben decided then that this was the time to leave that job and to do something else. In setting out to build his own company with other people Ben retrained his mind to follow more of his intuition through books, audio, role models and studied with some of the leaders of the personal-development field. He was then able to use both the initial training in structure he had received in his corporate roles and his new understanding of his own intuition, to be a more mindful leader.

It was not always an easy road for Ben. After leaving the corporate world he had a successful few years meeting targets and budgets, but when changes came in the economy, they came swiftly and the losses were too much for his small business to take. Ben therefore closed the business and went back to a corporate position in the printing industry. It was then another 12 months before he quit corporate again to work full time in creating a renewable energy business.

Very early on when establishing this new organisation, Ben was tested on what type of organisation ~ structured, mindful, or intuitive ~ it was going to be. The first test came up during advanced negotiations for the first product of the organisation. Ben and the other directors were meeting to discuss how to promote and distribute the product when the suppliers of the product, who had started to understand what was going to be the value added to their product, then requested better terms in the contract. This was agreed on and the contract sent back

CHAPTER 4: FEARLESSLY LETTING PASSION CREATE YOUR DAILY CALENDAR

to the suppliers. But when the suppliers received the contract they asked for further changes and better terms. At this point Ben and his fellow directors decided that the suppliers were just getting greedy and that this was not the type of relationship that they wanted to enter into, so they walked away from it.

Another test Ben faced was when, in the middle of a very large, important and lucrative deal, the client requested that Ben's team meet with the owner to discuss the terms. The owner turned out to be a very rude and arrogant person who was used to throwing his weight around. Ben reflected on this lesson at the time, and his approach was: "Of course we wanted the business but not at any cost".

In saying 'not at any cost' to suppliers and clients, Ben and his fellow founding directors were determining that they were going to be more mindful about the type of organisation they were building and the types of relationships they were going to be involved in. These tests, and many others like them, helped to clarify the personal and corporate boundaries of the types of lives that Ben and his directors were building and developing for themselves in this organisation. They were laying the groundwork for the DNA of a mindful organisation where, by using their structural technical skills and their intuitive personal skills, they were able to make mindful decisions for an overall positive result.

~ Ben Faiz, Managing Director Advanced ECO Solutions Pty Ltd

Review: key lessons in the mindful leadership Passion Step

- Passion is the energy that fuels activities in your life
- Understanding your unconscious programmes from childhood and other influences can assist you in changing them
- In doing activities, do them for yourself, for others and for your higher power
- Passion is essential for leaders to be able to define what to do so that they and their teams can align with it

To help integrate what has been covered in this chapter and to begin the journey of understanding Passion more in your life, consider the questions below.

Reflective questions

1. Are you leading the life you thought that you would be leading? Or is it a life that came out of other people's expectations?
   _____
   _____
   _____

2. How does your integrity determine what is acceptable or not acceptable to you?
   _____
   _____
   _____

3. In answering 2 what does it say about what you are passionate about doing in life, or not passionate about doing as well?
   _____
   _____
   _____

CHAPTER 4: FEARLESSLY LETTING PASSION CREATE YOUR DAILY CALENDAR

4. In communities or hobbies that you are involved in, how do they reflect your integrity and your passions?
_____
_____
_____

5. What in your current world does not match with your integrity but is accepted practice? What does this do to your passion for that activity? For life?
_____
_____
_____

PATHWAYS TO INTUITIVE DECISION-MAKING

Covered in this chapter:

• Definition of Pathways

• Why Pathways are important to know in decision-making

• The Pathways SIMPLE decision-making Model

• Why Pathways are essential for Leaders

• Interview: Martin Martinez
Chairperson The CEO Institute

"You can spend your whole life imagining ghosts, worrying about the pathway to the future. But all there will ever be is what's happening here and the decisions we make in this moment, which are based on either love or fear. So many of us choose our path out of fear disguised as practicality. What we really want seems impossibly out of reach and ridiculous to expect so we never dare to ask the universe for it.
I am saying I am the proof that you can ask the universe for it.
You can fail at what you don't want so you might as well take a chance on doing what you love." ~ Jim Carrey

Pathways are the directions that you use to fulfil your Purpose (why) and Passion (what), it is the how. In a business context it is the direction that is taken based on the decision-making of the leader. Decision-making is one of the key responsibilities of a leader and involves making the best choice of action in any given situation based on the information available. The action is then implemented and the pathway taken. The decision is made in that moment and is made with the intention to get the best outcomes possible.

A fundamental part of leadership involves the process of being the decision-maker in a situation. Yet how many leaders understand how they have come to a decision, or what it is about a decision that is making them feel uncomfortable and not wanting to commit to the decision at that time?

The model in Part One showing Structure and Intuition explains the two influencers of how decisions are made in the moment. On one side, decisions are made out of habits that have evolved and require no new awareness in that moment so that in a given situation the answer will be the same as it answer has always been. For example, many people always drink coffee with milk and one sugar and so do not think about drinking it differently each time. On the other side of the model, decisions are made out of intuition in each situation so that the answers could be different each time as there is no prescribed answer in that moment. For example, someone meeting an elephant for the first time may get some clues of the elephant's nature from observation, but ultimately would rely on intuition to decide whether to pat it or not.

Understanding how both habitual and intuitive decisions are made is required to be truly mindful in each moment. The skillset for mindful leaders is to develop their understanding of what they are doing out of habit (structure) and what they are doing intuitively (gut).

Gerd Gigerenzer, of the Maz Planck Institute for Human Development, published a book called *"Gut Feelings: The Intelligence of the Unconscious" (2007)* where he researched the essential steps in good decision-making. Gigerenzer concluded that the trick was not to amass information but to discard it by intuitively knowing what one doesn't need to know and that intuition or gut feelings "take advantage of certain capacities of the brain that have come down to us through time, experience and evolution."[8] He expanded on gut feelings, noting that they corresponded to neural processes that have evolved over thousands of years and give rise to usually sound decisions. A strong part of Gigerenzer's argument is that we would otherwise drown in a sea of information so hunches and facts are both equally valid. "It is possible to learn how to spot those situations and how to hone our intuition. Sometimes, however, the learning is in the school of hard knocks."[9]

Some examples of decision-making in a structured way

- meetings with agendas, action points and minutes
- reporting
- presentations

Some examples of decision-making in an intuitive way

- impromptu phone/email connections
- visiting colleagues unannounced
- listening to and hearing what is not being said in a conversation

Why understand the pathways to decision-making now?

With the increased speed of business and overwhelming volume of information available it is impossible for you to have all the right information required in that moment to be able to manage every situation that may arise. This can lead to a sense of overwhelm from not being able to access all the information required which increases stress and the sense you may have that you are failing more than ever to manage effectively.

Using a different mindset to this sense of overwhelm a mindful leader is aware that in life 'you are never given anything that you can't handle'. You are given the information and the situations that are just right for you at that point in time. Imagine how people like Gandhi or Mandela handled being persecuted while they were still leading their people and causes. With less information or social connectedness than we have today, these leaders still made decisions and managed the situations that they were involved in as they arose. His Holiness the Dalai Lama is another good example of someone leading people and situations by making decisions that impact on them in a mindful way.

In the same way that the decisions made by these famous people were right for them and their situations, the decisions of every leader within each of us, is right for the situation we are facing. This is a pivotal point in mindful leadership in understanding that when making a decision there is no wrong choice for you to make. Understanding how you are making the choice (structure or intuition) in the decision and connecting to that choice point is what is relevant. A leader who is connected to that moment and is fully mindful that they are making a choice, using the best that they are aware of from their habits, and their intuition, will not make the wrong choice for them.

There would be some who may argue that there can be wrong choices based on limited information, or inexperience, or many other seemingly valid reasons and in the industrial age some of this may have even been true. But the world has changed. In the digital age the more a person understands and accepts that they did the best they could in that moment, the better and more mindful a leader they will be.

The Pathways SIMPLE decision-making Model

In building on the model in Part One showing Structure and Intuition and how mindfulness is at the intersection of these two sides, the Pathways SIMPLE decision-making Model builds on the active choices and elements that are available in each moment that the decision itself is made.

Model 4. The Pathways SIMPLE decision-making Model

Structure   **Intuition**

▼ **Moment**
making the choice to use the structured or intuitive information available to you in that moment

● **Purpose**
checking how the decision is authentic for you and aligns with your purpose

♥ **Love**
using love and acceptance of yourself and trusting that this is the best decision you can make at this point in time

■ **Experience**
being grateful that all the experiences that have happened in your life were supporting you in making this decision in this moment now

Why is understanding this so important for leaders?

It is important for leaders to understand, accept and when needed, to change their pathways to decision-making because when not doing this, it results in their doing the same things over and over and still expecting different results. If they want to improve on those results then they need to become more aware of how they make their decisions in that moment.

CHAPTER 5: PATHWAYS TO INTUITIVE DECISION-MAKING

Over the last 30 years some of the biggest challenges that I have seen repeated in many organisational transformations reflected the lack of understanding of the choices available to the leaders in their decision-making. This showed up most in;

• Mismanagement of information about people's jobs. Many organisations were challenged by this as they would start by downsizing their HR department prior to a restructure and then spend all of their then limited HR capacity managing serious issues that they had created themselves by the restructure.

• Taking too long to explain the change and the reasons for it, to the staff involved. Staff were not only confused and angry about the change but were also lost as to why it is happening. The 'why is this happening to me' was on a bigger scale than if the organisational change was explained and the staff were able to understand the strategic reasons as to why they are being asked to be involved in that change.

So how could mindfulness about the decision-making have assisted in managing the organisational change so that they were managing it in a different way? In working with organisational change over a long period of time I noticed one common difference between leaders managing change successfully and those managing it less successfully. Success seemed to relate to the degree to which the leader was able to be more mindful by being able to empathise with the staff affected, which was then reflected in the decisions that they made. The Oxford dictionary defines empathy as "the ability to understand and share the feelings of another."

In determining whether staff would lose their jobs, change their jobs, or have to retrain to keep a job, the leader of the organisation worked to empathise and understand with each of the staff impacted. One example where this empathy worked well was in a Home Care organisation that I worked with, where we were selling and transferring part of their business operations to another organisation. This involved the transfer of over 500 staff with each of these staff having their own story to tell and motivators and reactions to what was going on. Some of the main reasons that this transfer of staff worked so successfully based on the decisions made by the leadership team were:

- it was determined early on which staff were transferring / changing / staying
- staff were advised as to which category they fitted into
- those that are not being asked to stay were advised of their options
- all staff were advised as to what would be happening when
- the implementation changes (changing contracts, giving redundancies, finalising end dates, etc.) happened very quickly
- all senior staff participated in managing any issues that arose

The same opportunities in decision-making were available to this organisation as to other organisations which have implemented changes less successfully. The difference with this organisation was that the leadership team were mindful about their decisions, had more empathy for their staff and the clients impacted and implemented their change activities based on this empathy in a quicker timeframe.

CHAPTER 5: PATHWAYS TO INTUITIVE DECISION-MAKING

Interview: ***The Intuitive Leader***

Martin credits his intuition as indispensable when he was making decisions that have led him to being a successful business leader. In using his intuition and learning from his biggest triumph, founding the Australian Poker League, he has learnt the lessons that business people learn in the school of hard knocks.

While living in a rational world where the numbers and markets may point to a particular decision as the one to make, Martin's approach differs in that he believes that every time he made a decision based on information alone, he has failed. By contrast, every time he made a decision based on his 'gut' he has succeeded. Intuition for Martin is based on his experience as a leader and in not overthinking things too much. So much so that in a meeting with a new person he can determine within the first 10 seconds whether or not he wants to do business or be associated with that person. This discernment about what works and what doesn't work for him comes from his trust in his own intuition. His decision-making, based on using his intuition, is his process for making decisions.

"I believe the awareness of leaders is heightened because they have a process where they are able to capture what is happening at an unconscious level and use this in decision-making. For me, this is my intuition, my gut, which I use to make decisions in my business and in my life." In leading businesses Martin made the best decisions that he could and if he had known how to do things better he would have done it differently. In being congruent with his beliefs like "not every dollar is worth getting", he also walks the talk that resonates with other people.

"Trust your gut and let it be your compass". Martin believes that people all have energies and vibes and even though this sounds very

woo woo, accepting it allows you to tap into it. In building successful businesses he has learnt not just how to be successful but also what not to do in business that works for him. It wasn't in boardroom meetings where he believes everyone just sits around that he was able to make decisions, but at times like walking the dog that the light bulb moments would come to him. It was in those moments when he felt or thought something when his best decisions were made. "It is choosing what is right for you because you are the only person who knows you. It is accepting and taking full ownership of who you are."

In leading by example Martin's mindful leadership style gives permission to those around him to also follow their own intuition. As a mentor to his clients and associates he is able to help these people at an even deeper level to connect into their own intuitive decisions that are congruent and right for them. He is genuinely a warm hearted man authentically leading and enlivening those around him.

~ Martin Martinez, Chairperson The CEO Institute

Review: key lessons in the mindful Pathways Step

- Pathways are the different decisions that you make, it is the 'how' part of life
- Understanding how you make a decision is important, is it structured or is it intuitive? How do you use information from both these areas?
- The Pathways SIMPLE (Structure, Intuition, Moment, Purpose, Love, Experience) decision-making Model
- To change the results of your decisions you need to change the how (the pathway) you use to make that decision

To help integrate what has been covered in this chapter and to begin the journey of understanding Pathways more in your life, consider the questions below.

Reflective Questions

1. When making decisions, are you aware when it is based on your habits (structured thinking) and when it is based on your intuition (your gut)?

_____
_____
_____

2. Can you see in others when they make decisions based on their habits (structured thinking) and when it is based on their intuition (their gut)?

_____
_____
_____

3. When you were given something that at the time you thought you couldn't handle, what happened afterwards?
___
___
___

4. How comfortable are you with your decisions after you have made them?
___
___
___

5. If there was one thing that you would do differently when making decisions, what would that be?
___
___
___

VALUING THE PEOPLE AND RELATIONSHIPS IN YOUR LIFE

Covered in this chapter:

• Definition of People

• Why it is important to value people in achieving the vision

• The Value Interaction Relationship Model

• Team Building for a shared vision

• Getting extra support to share the vision

• Interview: Lisa Chung AM
Chairperson The Front Project, NED Australian Unity, NED Artspace

> "The best executive is the one who has sense enough to pick good men to do what he wants done, and self-restraint enough to keep from meddling with them while they do it."
> ~ Theodore Roosevelt

In all areas of your life as a leader you interact with other people and in a much broader sense with the whole of humanity. In other words, you have a large sphere of influence. The Dalai Lama and the President of the United States are two examples of leaders with extensive spheres of influence and leadership, while the local football club president is also a leader and has their own, smaller sphere of influence.

The differences between the President of the United States and the footy club president arise from differences in their purpose, passion and pathway. The world, humanity, could not operate without each of these people following their own definition of purpose, passion and pathway in the world. Each is just as important and needed as the next, but they also cannot fulfil any of this on their own. You need others to form teams and alliances with you to be able to fulfil your destiny and the way to form together with other people is through a shared vision.

A shared vision (as opposed to mission, purpose, or strategic objective) is a future aspirational state that you wish to lead people to achieve in a cooperative way for the organisation. Examples of visions are: to be the leading brand, leading product, leading service, etc. Aligning your vision and those of your staff with the organisation's vision is critical to all being successful (win-win).

Research from Katherine Hyatt of Reinhardt University showed a significant positive correlation between leaders inspiring a shared vision and perceived organisational support. Her research supported earlier studies which had found that inspiring a shared vision had outcomes such as commitment, satisfaction, organisational performance and reduced turnover of staff. "These findings imply that developing and communicating a shared vision connects employees to the organisation which can lead to feelings of perceived support at work."[10] Hyatt further noted in her study that "Leaders' actions or behaviours reflect their feelings about employees and the organization as a whole."[11] This study confirms the vital importance of leadership practices which encourage employee commitment and perceived organizational support to performance.

So why is valuing the people who help you achieve the vision so important?

What type of leader, what type of person you are, is reflected in your values and the vision that you hold for the organisation. Every relationship comes down to the values that leaders show in their interactions with others. If staff, clients, vendors or shareholders are valued, then in the relationships with each of these people your attitude will be respectful and reflect that value. If you do not value them, then the relationships will also reflect this.

Do customers tell their friends about the wonderful service they received and that this is the best value for money they have ever had, or do they use social media to complain about the poor customer service they received instead? The value interaction relationship model below shows the interaction of these relationships further.

Model 5: The Value Interaction Relationship Model

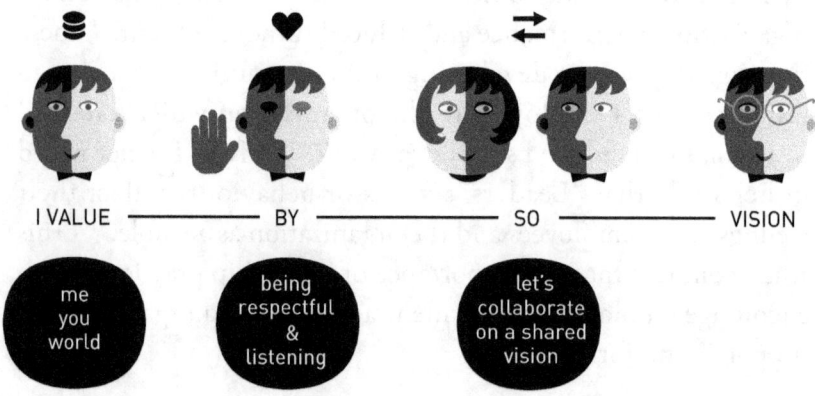

The first part of the model is where I have valued me. By understanding my purpose, passion and pathways I have then defined why I am here, what I am here to do and how I want to live my life. The interactions which I have with myself from then on are where I am putting this into action and reflect how I am valuing myself.

The second part of the model which shows how I am valuing others is where I am doing the same thing with them. I am listening to their purpose, passions and pathways and being respectful to what these are. This can also show me not only how well I have been able to understand these things for myself, but how well I have then been able to see them in others.

The third part of the model is how I am valuing the world. How am I understanding, in my world, what the purpose, passions and pathways are of the people, as a group around me, and being respectful to what these are? These questions assist in reflecting again how well I have been able to understand and see this in the world around me.

CHAPTER 6: VALUING THE PEOPLE AND RELATIONSHIPS IN YOUR LIFE

In being respectful and listening to these three areas you are creating the environment for everyone to come together and to collaborate on a shared vision. In valuing these different stakeholders (including yourself) you are creating a greater synergy of the individual parts from the team working on the vision as a whole group.

So how is this applied when leading a team and asking them to collaborate on a shared vision? People may be at different stages of the value interaction model and so it is necessary to understand where they are at when working with them. A useful way to understand where people are at on the model is by listening to them when they speak. If their language is saying things like "I did this, I completed that, I won…" then it may show that they have a low sense of value of themselves and are overcompensating with bravado. If their language is saying things like "he did this, he completed that, he won…" then it may be that they have an undervalued sense of self when compared to others or to their place in the world.

Or the person may have a good value of themselves and just be genuinely complimenting others when they speak in this way. In team building there will be different people with different levels of valuing themselves and others. You will need to be respectful of this and to listen actively to where they are at. By identifying where they are at, and using terms that are meaningful to them you will be able to engage them more in what you are asking them to do. Your intuition would be another useful tool in these situations. As Sir Richard Branson observed:

> *"A company is people… employees want to know… am I being listened to or am I a cog in the wheel? People really need to feel wanted."* [12]

Getting extra support to share the vision

There are a number of ways to get extra support to share the vision when building a team. Some of the main methods are through mentoring, coaching and creating a team of vision champions.

Mentoring is where you are working with someone who has more experience than you and who is assisting you to learn how to do things differently. It may also be where you are the experienced person and you are helping someone more junior to you. The process of gaining insights from someone more experienced, or from the naivety of someone with less experience ~ two ends of the same spectrum ~ helps you to define and develop the vision.

Business coaching is a very popular tool used by leaders as an independent sounding board for their ideas and to work through some of the complexities that they may face. A coach can be an invaluable tool to bounce ideas off as they will have had extensive experience in working with other leaders in similar situations as to how best to build a team to take a vision forward.

In building a team and engaging people on a shared vision it will bring forward a range of responses from those people to that vision. In change management, the people who support a change programme are often utilised as change champions. In a similar way leaders can build their vision champions as the main people within the organisation who also lead and champion the vision. The more people who are engaged in building the vision and holding it as part of their leadership role, the more likely the business is to be successful in achieving it.

CHAPTER 6: VALUING THE PEOPLE AND RELATIONSHIPS IN YOUR LIFE

Interview: ***The Relationship Leader***

As a senior lawyer, board chairperson, mother and volunteer Lisa is a very relationship-driven person and it forms an underlying theme in all that she does. She believes that everyone has an interesting story in them and that the secret to the quality of your life is in the relationships that you form with people.

As a lawyer, it is about the relationships in the journey with clients and colleagues in delivering the commercial and other outcomes that they seek. As a mother, it is about setting up her kids to realise the importance of relationships, especially the one they have with themselves. As chairperson on a board or a volunteer in a drop-in centre, it is participating in this 'secret' of the incomparable riches you receive in your relationships when giving back to others in society.

The most fulfilment that Lisa has experienced in her professional career has been in the development of younger lawyers. "Law firms are 100% people organisations and yet are notoriously poor at managing their people. I was fascinated by this dynamic and so try to make a difference through strategically training and supporting the best lawyers. It is important to not only attract the best people but to also retain them."

In giving back so much of her time and energy to support others, Lisa stresses that the main thing to being a successful leader is to know yourself, and from this self-awareness make adjustments as opportunities arise. In making these types of active decisions about your career and opportunities you are developing your critical thinking which is an important skill for any type of decision making.

As an accomplished leader in many areas, Lisa learnt very early the difference between 'who-ness' and 'what-ness'. She defines these

terms as "the 'what-ness' being that you are the CEO of x, and the 'who-ness' being who you are if they took the 'what-ness' away from you and you looked at what was left." She goes on: "If there is not much substantial left behind, then you are in a very bad place and need to do something about it."

Law firms typically don't have a command and control hierarchical structure as they are notionally all equals at the management level. "Law firms have been a good training ground in 'who-ness' because in today's world you can't just command and control people to do things for you. It's very much about bringing people along with you and it's about influencing them to trust you and your judgement in leading them, by building relationships with each of them."

These relationships are critical for leaders as they hold the vision that the organisation is working towards. By articulating the vision, engaging people in it, and implementing and leading people through it, the leader is demonstrating this 'who-ness'. Only in this way can the leader line up their own leadership style with the tone, cultures and behaviours for the organisation to be successful.

~ *Lisa Chung AM, Chairperson The Front Project, NED Australian Unity, NED Artspace*

CHAPTER 6: VALUING THE PEOPLE AND RELATIONSHIPS IN YOUR LIFE

Review: key lessons in the mindful leadership People Step

- People are who you interact with as a leader in all areas of your life, not just in work situations
- A shared vision is how business leaders lead people
- The Value Interaction Relationship Model shows how people value relationships to themselves, to others and to the world
- Leading a team to collaborate on a shared vision you need to be respectful and listen to where they are at and to what is important to them
- Mentoring can assist in giving more support and expertise whilst also building relationships

To help integrate what has been covered in this chapter and to begin the journey of understanding People more in your life, consider the questions below.

Reflective questions

1. What is your vision for you? For your organisation?

_____

_____

_____

2. How do you value yourself, the people and the world around you?

_____

_____

_____

3. How do you build relationships, build teams of people?
_____
_____
_____

4. What type of language do you need to use to collaborate with your team? How can you engage them on a shared vision?
_____
_____
_____

5. List three people that you will talk to about your vision and how you are going to get people on board with your vision. Think about who you choose and why, and reflect on whether these people could become mentors for you or you for them.
_____
_____
_____

GIVING CREATES PROSPERITY AND MAKES YOU HANDSOME

Covered in this chapter:

- What is Prosperity?

- The Cycle of Giving and Receiving

- The Giving and Receiving Model

- Why it is important to give back as a Leader

- Interview: Ruth Medd
Chairperson Women on Boards

> *"We make a living by what we get.*
> *We make a life by what we give."*
> ~ Winston S. Churchill

Prosperity encompasses not only the area of monetary wealth but also health, happiness, social relationships and much more. Many times some of these elements are seen to be almost contradictory to each other but ask the person with poor health whether they would like more money or better health, or ask the person without much money if they would prefer money to good social relationships. So it is a mixture of these elements which may have different levels of relative importance for each person, which determines what they then define as prosperity.

The cycle of giving and receiving appears in different forms in different cultures. It relates back to the concept that everything is energy and to keep the energy flowing (and fresh) it is just as important to give as it is to receive and to receive as it is to give. The most commonly-used example is the Dead Sea bordering Jordan, Israel and the West Bank. The reason that the sea is dead is that the rivers flow into the sea but the sea itself does not flow out anywhere else. Most rivers have tributaries that flow into and out of them over their length. The Amazon for example, the greatest river of South America, enters Brazil at one-fifth the water flow that it then discharges out into the Atlantic on the other side of Brazil.[13] The rivers that flow into the Dead Sea finish their journeys there, whilst the waters that flow into the Amazon flow in and out all the way along it until it reaches its final destination at the Atlantic.

This concept of giving back is also known as the 'paying it forward' idea. I have had people in my life be very generous with time and money and used to feel like I should be repaying them personally for what I received, until I realised that I was performing the same role for other people in my life, and that there was a bigger picture of giving and receiving going on. When I realised this I became more attuned to where I could pay it forward and appreciate those opportunities more.

The Giving and Receiving Model

The elements of giving and receiving can best be viewed in the model below where it is seen as a continuous flow and what the person in the centre of the model receives is ongoing prosperity. In the context of human civilization and dating back to agrarian times, giving in the form of sacrifices was made to the God of that culture as a part of a seasonal celebration. So mankind has been participating in some form of 'giving back' throughout history.

Model 6: The Giving and Receiving Model

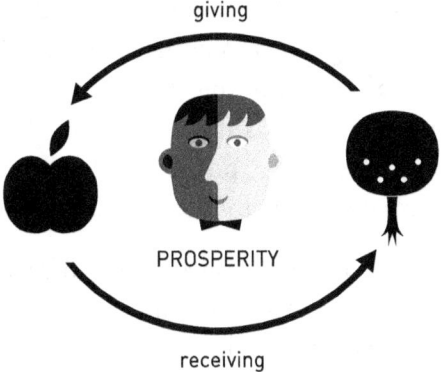

Driving your car provides a good example of the everyday process of giving and receiving. There are times when driving that you need to receive (others let you in their lane) and then later on you have opportunities to give (letting others into your lane). Yes, there are drivers who never let anyone into their lane and others who seem to let everyone in. Without knowing their stories it is not possible to know whether this is that person's moment of paying it forward or not, so it is not about judging this, it is about understanding that in that moment the person may or may not be conscious of what is going on and that they may be paying it forward somewhere else in their lives.

Arthur C. Brooks, President of the American Enterprise Institute, in his Wall Street Journal article "Handsome is As Handsome Gives" notes that charitable giving boosts our health, our happiness, and even our attractiveness to others. He quotes a study from 2009 where "Dutch and British researchers showed female college students one of three videos featuring the same handsome actor. In the first, he gives generously to a beggar on the street; in the second, he hands over just a little money; and in the third, the man gives nothing. The more he gave, the more handsome he appeared to the women in the study."[14] In an earlier study that Brooks completed called "Does Giving Make Us Prosperous" he identified that there is strong evidence that giving money does in fact influence income. "The implication of these findings for researchers and managers is that the value of charity is not limited to those who receive the services that giving makes possible. On the contrary, charity unleashes substantial benefits to the givers themselves."[15]

The second part of the model is receiving which is required just as much as the first part of giving to balance it out. For some people there is a very real uncomfortableness about receiving whether it is receiving something as simple as a compliment or positive feedback and yet being open to this is important for the whole flow of energy in the prosperity cycle. Sometimes the protective walls you place around yourself from the 'bad' out there can then also stop you from being able to receive the 'good'. It can take practice to become more open to receiving and to allow more into your life. In the previous driving example when you are being let into a lane when driving this is an everyday example of when you have been open to receive. Daily life provides many other opportunities to practice and to keep opening up to receiving the prosperity in your life.

Why is it important to give back as a leader?

As a leader you will be able to find many ways in which to determine how to give back from the income that the organisation receives (keeping in mind that the money is like the river flowing into the bank account then out again into the sea). In many organisations giving back can take the form of pro-bono work or specific funding to designated charities. Through identifying what service your organisation can do, perform or sponsor you can then give back according to the nature and size of your organisation. Another practical example is with flexible work arrangements which allow people to work from home or to work unusual hours. The organisation thus gives back to its staff by offering optional work styles, a practice that is also congruent in a workplace which encourages flexible thinking in its staff. Flexible working arrangements can in this way align with the values of the organisation which promotes flexibility and freedom of thought.

For some organisations due to the products or services that they create these types of flexible work arrangements would not be practical. A production line may need a mechanical engineer close by in case of a breakdown, the police or emergency services need to be physically present in situations they are responding to like an accident. For these organisations flexible working arrangements for staff may not suit and so there are different ways that the organisation can give back in alignment with their values.

Charitable organisations are good examples where the values of the organisation are reflected in the values of the staff who in some form or another personally live and reflect those values both inside and outside the workplace. The charity itself in some form asks its staff members to give back to their clients and the staff members willingly do so. This may take the form of voluntary work, unpaid representation, and other activities that are outside the job description for that role.

Keeping the form of giving back central to all organisational activities can be a delicate step as there is a fine line between communicating giving-back activities and false advertising to stakeholders as to what is being done. That is why it is crucial that the form of giving back aligns with the organisational values. If it does not align then it may come across as insincere and as a corporate gimmick.

Giving back as a leader develops within you the generosity of spirit that then makes you an even more influential leader. Giving with no expectations or strings attached also develops a sense of freedom with what you give. A leader acting and behaving in this way also demonstrates these qualities for others. In the movie Avatar there was an expression that was used when the Na'vis on the planet Pandora greeted each other, which was, "I see you". In the Pandoran culture this meant that the person they were meeting with saw not just the superficial outer parts of them but was also connecting on a deeper level with the essence of who they were. Imagine the effect that this genuine connection would have, if you were to practice it with your staff and colleagues. The only cost in your interactions would be the investment of time and focus but the return in such investments would be immense.

When staff have been hired to align their values with the DNA

CHAPTER 7: GIVING CREATES PROSPERITY AND MAKES YOU HANDSOME

of your organisation, and therefore represent it, then asking for their suggestions, in terms of determining what products, service and time to give back, is the most effective method in determining how to give back. Giving back can apply to all stakeholders of an organisation, for example:

- Customers - discounts for pensioners, social card holders
- Staff - flexible work arrangements, paid study, service
- Shareholders - commissioned industry reports as to how the industry sector is going
- Management - paid leave, study opportunities
- Community - sponsorship, pro-bono work, access to facilities

Many large organisations may also set up separate funds or trusts to manage the giving back activities. This can be an efficient way of managing those activities when their value is more substantial. They can then become organisations in their own right, fundraising on their own and then using these larger bodies of funds for bigger activities. The Bill and Melinda Gates Foundation is an example of this type of organisation which has received over $46.8 billion in donations towards its work.

- When I was completing a 28-day leadership training program in the US, part of the requirement for our graduation was that we organise and deliver school materials for needy families within 24 hours. This had been a long and gruelling course with one day off out of 28 and at the end of it we were then asked to dig a bit deeper again with yet another task. We all rose to the challenge and planned and delivered a successful event. Each of us would also express that the small part that we played in being of service to our fellow human beings left us feeling very

> humbled indeed. There really wasn't any price that you could put on the joy of the children's faces when they received those basic school materials and of their parents gratitude for acts of kindness.

So don't deny your staff or yourself the opportunity to really be of service and to experience that connection with other human beings by being of service in whatever way that you can. Most people who have been of service in any way will explain how the amount of time, money and resources used paled in comparison with the innate sense of joy felt when seeing the people receiving the goods or services.

CHAPTER 7: GIVING CREATES PROSPERITY AND MAKES YOU HANDSOME

Interview: *The Inspirational Leader*

Building a community and inspiring women to take their next steps as a Director in their careers is Ruth's latest mission. In different ways, either as a facilitator in a workshop, a speaker at an event, or one-on-one, her generosity with time and energy in working with people to help them reach their highest potential is inspirational.

As an advocate and strategist for women's issues for a number of years, Ruth has been instrumental in changing many people's lives. A firm believer in giving women a better lot at the top end of town, she supports women in establishing the infrastructure needed and facilitating this through the organisations and groups she is involved with. Ruth works tirelessly on regulatory, reporting and other advocacy roles to create cultural change and equality for women. "Until the people at the top of organisations see the value of diversity then nothing will happen."

One of the ways that Ruth supports and inspires women is by working with them on their steps to getting a position on an appropriate board. By helping them identify what they have to offer the world and what their strengths and transferable skills are, she can tangibly help them to get clearer about what they have to offer, she inspires them to see that the board position they are seeking is possible.

She believes that while leadership may have once been about telling people what to do, it is now about inspiring them to do it. For her, inspiring people, whether one-on-one or in groups, is her way of giving back to people of her time, experience and insights. Ruth is vivacious in her energy and enthusiasm and sees herself as being like a tap, turning on inspiration as opportunities arise to assist and mentor others.

In a very grounded way she sees that many women who want to go onto boards do so because they see opportunities to generously give back and help others, especially by working with a not-for-profit organisation. Ruth can assist women to determine whether this is the best move for them or if a paid role in a commercial organisation is a better choice for them to give of their time.

Ruth, when looking at someone like Rupert Murdoch who is still going and doesn't seem likely to stop anytime soon, can see similarities in how she as a natural adventurer will also keep moving on and finding the next inspirational activity for years to come. For in understanding how fortunate she has been in her own life, she can see that she will continue to turn on that inspiration tap, and give of herself from this gift to others.

~ Ruth Medd, Chairperson Women on Boards

CHAPTER 7: GIVING CREATES PROSPERITY AND MAKES YOU HANDSOME

Review: key lessons in the mindful leadership Prosperity Step

- Prosperity is having a mixture of elements like wealth, health and social relationships, etc.
- Giving is the same as paying it forward
- The Giving and Receiving Model shows how this is an ongoing process for prosperity in all areas of life
- It is important to give back as a leader in practical ways to all your stakeholders
- Connect with others like a Na'vis (from the movie Avatar) would, 'I see you'
- Give back in ways that align with your purpose

To help integrate what has been covered in this chapter and to begin the journey of understanding Prosperity more in your life, consider the questions below.

Reflective questions

1. Where is it that you give in your life (time, money, effort)?
_____
_____
_____

2. Where is it that you receive in your life (time, money, effort)?
_____
_____
_____

3. Are there areas that seem a bit like the Dead Sea in that you receive more than you give?
_____
_____
_____

4. Are there areas in which it seems like you give more than you receive?
_____
_____
_____

5. If there was one area of service to humanity, to the planet, that you could do in your life what would it be and how can you do it?
_____
_____
_____

BEING MINDFUL TO THE PAUSING MOMENTS BETWEEN EACH BREATH

Covered in this chapter:

• What is Pausing?

• The Pausing Model for Focusing the Mind

• Mindful Movement

• Mindful Stillness

• Interview: Neil Thompson
CEO Velocity Frequent Flyer

> *"The right word may be effective, but no word was ever as effective as a rightly timed pause."*
> ~ Mark Twain

Pausing is the act of taking time out from what you are doing, thinking about or feeling, to spend time in just being. This is typically done through some form of meditative activity where there is a conscious choice to stop and only focus on one thing for a period of time. It can be as simple as the act of pausing to consider the next words or actions before speaking and in that moment of reflection, consciously focusing on what your next words or actions will be. It is in that reflection that pausing brings complete focus to the moment.

For many leaders the demands of a 24/7 working life mean that the practice of pausing and taking time from the stresses that they are experiencing can seem too difficult to do when there is so much going on that requires their attention. This is where their health and relationships can suffer and it can become a continuous cycle where their increased stress levels mean that they are not managing very well, which then creates more work for them to complete.

Research by the University of California, Berkeley, has shown that chronic stress can generate long-term changes in the brain and affect learning and memory. Long term chronic stress can also increase the risk of chronic obesity, heart disease and depression. The research showed that although some acute stress (that is short lived) may be good for people to push them through to their next level of performance, it is the ongoing chronic stress that can negatively affect people.

CHAPTER 8: BEING MINDFUL TO THE PAUSING MOMENTS BETWEEN EACH BREATH

The Pausing Model for Focusing the Mind

The pausing model uses a combination of mind focusing and releasing steps to train the mind to focus on one thing in the moment. It is through the application of each of these steps that the mind is able to release what it is holding onto, quieten or calm down and then focus.

Model 7: The Pausing Model for Focusing the Mind

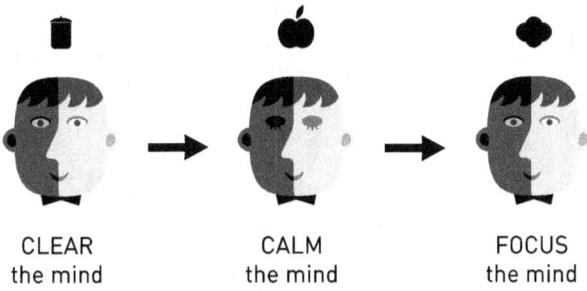

Clear the mind

Pausing starts with clearing the mind. Anything urgent or important is captured so that it does not need to be worried about or remembered by the mind. It is a very powerful way of clearing the mind and can be useful later as it generates a 'to do' list. The way to clear the mind of information is to allocate some time to sit with pen and paper and write down everything that comes up in your mind. This process of mind clearing has also been called a mind dump.

Once this list of items has been downloaded from your mind, the next step can be to categorise them. This can be done immediately after writing the list, or later on (after focusing the mind). The crucial point is to first get this list of things out of the mind and onto paper.

If categorising the list at this stage then the next part is to break the list of activities into three groups based on expected time it would take to complete each of them:

- Activities that take no more than 5 minutes
- Activities that take no more than 1-2 hours
- Activities that take longer than 2 hours

With the activities that would only take up to 5 minutes, allocate a time when you are able to do these and then sit down, focus your attention and only do these activities in that time that you have allocated.

With the activities that would take between 1-2 hours, allocate times for when you will complete these but also allocate time to take a break after each task. Also see whether there are some activities that require other things to happen first so that you can work out the most practical sequence.

Think of the activities that are going to take over 2 hours to complete as individual projects from small to big. You may need to work out a plan of how to complete each of them and you may also need other people to help get them done. With these larger activities, prioritise them in order of urgency.

With these lists of things from your mind grouped into the 3 areas, you will begin to feel lighter and more energised as you will not be trying to remember everything. With this now clearer mind and list of tasks or activities, with completion times against each, it is time to calm the mind by choosing a microscopic step.

Calm the mind with microscopic steps

When looking at your list of activities from your mind it can seem very daunting or complicated and even as if there will never be a time when it will be finished. It can seem overwhelming at the beginning of it but as the Chinese philosopher Lao-Tzu has said, "Every journey of a thousand miles starts with a single step."[16] The same is true for any activity undertaken.

So what is a microscopic step then? It is when the focus is on doing something that is very small, a small part of a step, as the preparation to taking even that step. The idea with a microscopic step is that it is something very simple and very easy to do.

An example of a microscopic step may be checking the phone number of somebody that you will call later or getting out books that you are going to sort out at a later time. The major point to understand is that you are taking a small action towards the completion of a bigger step or task.

Another good example is in the area of health and fitness. Many people decide to get healthy and set up grand plans and ideas as to what they would like to achieve. They start some activities like dieting and exercising daily and then very soon it all becomes too hard so they stop and don't continue on with any of it at all. In many ways they have been too ambitious too quickly.

If they had instead begun with a microscopic step, say moving for at least 5 minutes a day, then that is something that they could easily do each day. Because it would not become too hard, as it is so small to do, it could become a part of their everyday activities. So, similar to the daily brushing of your teeth, this microscopic step of moving for 5 minutes a day could become part of your daily routine as well. The success of accomplishing these smaller achievable steps allows people to believe that the bigger goals are achievable as well. Then very soon they start to believe that they can finish those thousand miles (those activities) that they have started out to do.

So with the current task list that you have created in front of you, determine which of these, or part of these, is going to be a microscopic step. Once you have picked something, check with yourself that this microscopic step really is achievable, and one that seems most urgent to you at that time.

This microscopic step then becomes the essential activity to calming the mind as you have now agreed with yourself what the next step for your activities is. So if anything else comes to mind in that moment it can be dismissed as it is not your next step at this time. Later on you can return to the whole list and work out what is required to complete the rest of it and which bits can also be broken down into more microscopic steps.

Focusing of the mind

The final step now the mind has been cleared and calmed, is through the practice of focusing it on one thing, such as the breath going in and out of body. Below are examples for focusing the mind by either moving or staying still as the practice itself can be applied to any activity and at any time when the mind is being focused on a single task.

Mindful movement

When you are moving around during the day, for much of the time you are not that conscious or aware of what you are doing or what is happening with your body. This is especially true when

CHAPTER 8: BEING MINDFUL TO THE PAUSING MOMENTS BETWEEN EACH BREATH

you are knocking into things and stubbing your toes, etc. Mindful movement is the practice of moving your body whilst focusing on it. Some martial arts, dance and physical therapy disciplines combine focus and movement as a part of their techniques. Nia, Feldenkrais, Yoga and Karate are examples of this. These all use the focus of the mind and the movement of the body in a structured way. Whether it is through martial arts or some form of everyday movement, the practice of bringing your mind to that movement is like doing exercise in the gym. The more that you practice it the better you get. In a similar way you can connect for example to the food that you are eating and the feelings from walking on different surfaces like grass compared to concrete. In noticing these differences and being mindful of them, you are training your mind to discern how your body handles these different experiences.

The focusing of the mind on the moving of the body is something that people automatically do when they have injured a part of their body, but rarely do when all the body parts are working well. Focusing on the movement of a part of the body when it is working well helps to attune you to what this feels like.

Mindful walking is also a powerful way of bringing focus into the moment. Have you ever stopped and asked yourself: how did I get here? Did you last remember being somewhere and then when you focused on where you were again, realised that you had walked somewhere and not realised it? Or had a conversation with someone and been walking along and not noticed the scenery or the passing time, and arrived at your destination surprised that you were now there?

All of these actions indicate that your mind or focus has been elsewhere and not on the activity of walking and being observant of the journey as you were walking. In mindful walking the opposite is true and you are aware of each moment in the journey as you are walking. The first thing that you would notice is the scenery changing as you are walking along. The sights, sounds and experience of the environment are heightened as you are now tuned into these parts of the walk. The weather ~ noticing if it is sunny, cold, windy, hot ~ is also now a part of the walk being taken.

The experiences of your body as you are tuning into the walk will become more noticeable. As there is a focus on moving your legs and arms the sensations become clearer and more noticeable. If there are aches, pains, or tension in parts of your body, these areas also become more noticeable. As you begin focusing more on the walk itself your thoughts also become less noticeable and drop away. This training of focusing on one thing, the mindful walking practice, becomes a way of expanding this type of mental focus into other areas of your life as well. There is a popular expression about the need in life to stop and smell the roses every now and then. This is very similar to the idea of stopping and being present when you are walking, and enjoying the journey that you are on.

Mindful stillness

The practice of mindful stillness is regularly used by those who sit in meditation for a period of time. Meditation refers to a range of practices that are designed to develop concentration, promote relaxation and clarity, and to slow down and bring awareness to the thoughts in your mind. Thoughts cannot easily be stopped so the point of meditation is to instead bring focus and stillness to these thoughts.

There are many types of meditation that people practice, the main ones being:

Religious and spiritual meditations

Bahá'í Faith – In Bahá'í teachings, meditation and prayer are both primary tools for spiritual development and mainly refer to one's reflection on the words of God.

Buddhism – Buddhist meditative practices are associated with religion and philosophy and part of the path to enlightenment. There are numerous meditation schools within Buddhism, each with a large number of practices for focusing the mind using different mindfulness, concentration or visualisation techniques.

Christianity – Christian meditation is a term for a form of prayer in which a structured attempt is made to get in touch with, and to deliberately reflect upon, the revelations of God.

Taoism – Taoist meditation has a long history, and like Buddhism, has developed various techniques such as concentration, visualisation and mindfulness meditations.

Hinduism – Meditation is widely practised by followers of Hinduism. There are many schools and styles of meditation within Hinduism, all designed to assist in uniting one's self with God.

Islam also has different meditative techniques, and the reason behind each is the remembrance of God. In some forms, e.g. Sufism, it may include control breathing and the chanting of holy words.

Sikhism – In Sikhism, simran (meditation) and good deeds are both necessary to achieve spiritual goals, so without good deeds meditation is futile. When Sikhs meditate they aim to feel God's presence and immerse themselves in the divine light.

Jainism* meditation involves a number of meditation techniques that aim at realizing the self, attaining salvation and taking the soul to complete freedom.

Judaism - Meditative practices in Judaism are believed to go back thousands of years and particularly in the Kabbalah schools, where the purpose of meditation is to understand and connect with the Divine.

New Age meditations are often influenced by Eastern philosophy, mysticism, Yoga, Hinduism and Buddhism and sometimes also contain a degree of Western influence. They have evolved into a range of practices ranging from a focus on realms of consciousness through to the concentration of energy in group meditation.

Pagan and Occult Religions - There are numerous movements which use meditation as an entry into occult or magical practices. In these movements, meditation usually takes the form of visualisation through directing of energy and the inducing of trance states.

Prayer Beads - Most of the ancient religions of the world have a tradition of using some type of prayer beads as tools in devotional meditation. Most prayer beads and Christian rosaries consist of pearls or beads linked together by a thread.

Secular Meditation (i.e. not religious or spiritually based)

Mindfulness Meditation - There are different practices that can be used in mindfulness meditations. Popular ones are those that can be used in daily life through focusing on everyday activities such as being aware of the taste and texture of the food eaten.

CHAPTER 8: BEING MINDFUL TO THE PAUSING MOMENTS BETWEEN EACH BREATH

One person who integrated his meditation practices of yoga and Buddhism with his scientific background was Jon Kabat-Zinn, the founder of the Mindfulness-Based Stress Reduction (MBSR) program, from the University of Massachusetts Medical Center. The MBSR program, initially designed to assist people in a hospital setting, uses a combination of meditation, body awareness, and yoga to help people become more mindful. His research has found that regular meditation has a positive effect on brain function, anxiety, pain and even such ailments as psoriasis. Through repetition, the state induced in the brain can become a personality trait and is reflected in long-term changes to the brain functions and structure.[17]

By participating in a particular approach to meditation you can connect with how your mind works and how to train your mind into new ways of being. With regular practice using a meditation technique can completely transform your mind and your relationship to it.

By using either mindful movement, mindful stillness or combinations of both, you can take those moments of pausing to recharge your energy, focus your energy and release what you don't need in that moment. By letting go, breathing and pausing to focus only on that moment you can truly just be in that moment and all of the richness in meaning and joy that moment can bring to you.

Interview - **The Conduit Leader**

As a linguist at heart Neil started his career working as a translator and this foundation has been what he has taken with him through each subsequent role since. The skills he learnt around communication, relationships and pausing before responding, matched and honed his own natural abilities to work as a conduit in utilising both his structured and intuitive skills.

Communication is important as leading a team requires the management of dynamic tensions for example, the balance of the tensions between being honest and being willing to express hard truths or, between being empathic and listening to people. He believes it is the "constant balancing of the polarities, the two ends of the spectrum, and knowing which side to be in at which point in time".

Relationships are important for Neil and need to be grounded in trust, respect and openness. Dealing with people he sees himself as building relationships as opposed to purely conducting transactions. These elements are important to enable the room for structure and intuition to be used by all parties involved. This intuition Neil has also utilised in organisations where "truthfulness was not always the predominant value" and where he was not able to be authentic.

Neil sees the pausing before responding as a foundation of mindfulness and the difference between reacting and responding. "Mindfulness encapsulates that you are moving out of reaction (being mindless) where you are reacting to a stimulus of some sort and responding instead in a mindful way. In pausing you are opening up to the other elements of what are in the interaction, the bigger context." All that this takes is a momentary shift out

CHAPTER 8: BEING MINDFUL TO THE PAUSING MOMENTS BETWEEN EACH BREATH

of your reaction to the stimulus by taking a breath, looking away, or some other way of pausing before you then respond. In a world of social connectedness where you are always on when leading teams and when working for people, this moment of pausing prior to responding is key to decision making.

In reflecting on role models in his own life Neil can see that those who made an impression on him were the ones who were able to be present in the moment and modelled for him the way that he wanted to treat and be treated by others. "They had a way of being that emanated from them of being absolutely present in the moment when you were with them."

As a conduit for people, ideas and information, Neil is a truly mindful leader who also gives of his skills through mentoring and work in the not for profit sector. Neil believes that while it is human to "fall off the wagon 100 times a day", practising mindfulness requires us to get back up and hone those skills some more.

~ Neil Thompson, CEO Velocity Frequent Flyer

Review: key lessons in the mindful leadership Pausing Step

- Pausing is taking time out from what you are doing, thinking or feeling
- The Pausing Model for focusing the mind involves clearing the mind, calming the mind and then focusing the mind
- Mindful movement is when the mind is completely focused on the movement of the body in some way e.g. walking
- Mindful stillness is when the mind is completely focused on the stillness of the body, mind and emotions, and is usually achieved through some form of meditation

To help integrate what has been covered in this chapter and to begin the journey of understanding Pausing more in your life, consider the questions on the next page.

Reflective questions

1. How do you take time out from what you are doing, thinking or feeling?
_____
_____
_____

2. List three microscopic steps that you can take to achieve the most important things that you want to do in your life at the moment. What is stopping you from taking these steps?
_____
_____
_____

CHAPTER 8: BEING MINDFUL TO THE PAUSING MOMENTS BETWEEN EACH BREATH

3. Have you taken a walk and not noticed how you got from A to B? What could have helped you to be more mindful on that walk?
   _____
   _____
   _____

4. What is the longest that you have been able to sit quietly for? What supported you to be able to sit quietly for that length of time?
   _____
   _____
   _____

5. If there was one thing that would assist in you pausing each day what is it? What microscopic step can you take to make it happen?
   _____
   _____
   _____

PRESENCE IS BEING DRESSED FROM WITHIN

Covered in this chapter:

• What is Presence?

• The Presence Model

• Why it is important to have Presence as a Leader

• Brand Me

• Interview: Danielle Lehrer
Founder Forex Nation, RAC Advisory Board Member

> *"As we let our light shine, we unconsciously*
> *give other people permission to do the same.*
> *As we are liberated from our own fear,*
> *our presence actually liberates others."*
> ~ Marianne Williamson

Presence is that undefinable something that causes everyone in a room to sit up and take notice when you walk into a room. It will not be because you are doing anything that is drawing attention to yourself but because of an air that you carry about you. Anything that you say is listened to, anything that you recommend becomes the thing to do and even people who don't know you find themselves genuinely liking you.

Many movie stars and famous people have this quality of presence, partly because members of the public have created the aura around them and partly because they are used to being the centre of attention. This generally comes from the role that the person is playing at that time, which means it sometimes ends with the role, so it is only a temporary presence. More permanent presence is something that some people are born with and may be learned by others.

The Presence Model looks at the elements that create presence and helps to explain why some people have a stronger presence than others. The good news is that whatever your level of presence is, it can be improved upon.

Model 8: The Presence Model

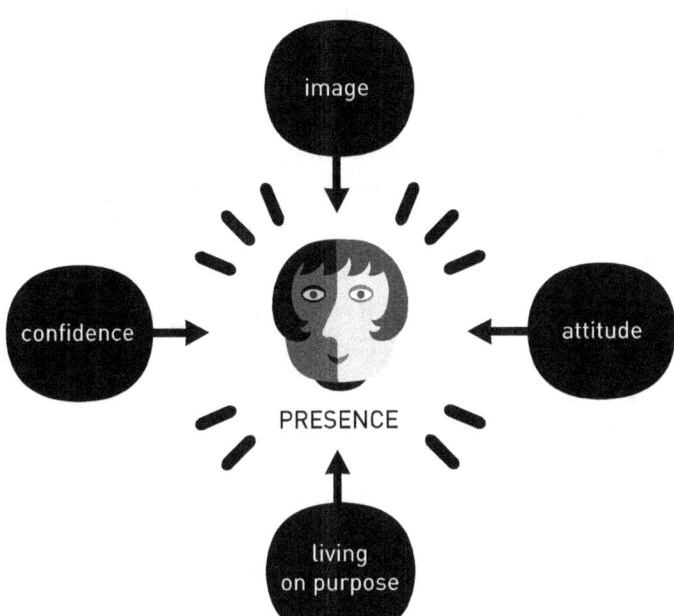

Image

The first thing that people notice about anyone is how they look. Some people look crisper and smarter than others. Your image also says a lot about how well you respect and take care of yourself so if your clothes have holes or stains, it suggests that you are not taking care of yourself. Your hair is also a reflection of this. It is not the shape, length or style of your hair but the way it has been brushed, combed or maintained. Other personal grooming is an extension of this so if your teeth are yellow or your makeup is too loud, it may indicate low self-respect.

If you are well groomed, nicely dressed and show that you have taken care of the things that you are wearing then you will receive more respect. Having a personal style that reflects you and your personality can also enhance this. This is not about having the richest or the best clothes, hair, makeup etc. It is about making the most of what you do have.

As a leader the gaining of respect from how you dress is a vital tactical move in presenting your image. Different industries may encourage different dress codes (IT workers generally wear jeans whilst many bankers prefer suits). So if you are a banker and do decide to wear jeans, the jeans would not be ripped or low-slung and other status symbols like an expensive designer watch would be used to maintain your high level of personal status and grooming.

Confidence

A person with presence may seem larger than they are as they seem to fill more space. Any possible perception of arrogance in their behaviour is balanced by their showing a genuine interest in the people around them. A good posture is another of the ways that confidence is portrayed to those around you. People with poor posture appear less confident and knowledgeable than those with good posture, who look like they are in control and know what they are doing.

Leaders with presence also have a commanding tone of voice and intonation that indicates that they know and understand what is going on, even when they say they don't. It is the confidence with which you are speaking and projecting your voice which gives you this presence. It is also the authenticity with which you are speaking and inviting people to participate that adds to your appeal. Through this openness and invitation to be part of something other than just their functional role in an organisation, you are asking people to contribute in an even bigger way which can be very compelling.

CHAPTER 9: PRESENCE IS BEING DRESSED FROM WITHIN

Attitude

Presence can come across as either a positive or a negative (arrogant) attitude towards others. The difference lies in how you present yourself to others. If the conversations are all one way and you are distracted, staff will not feel connected to you at all. If you take the time to establish eye contact and listen to what the staff have to say then they will feel connected. By asking questions and making staff members feel appreciated, and valued by the organisation, you will genuinely be respected.

Attitude cannot be faked and so if it is not in your personality to connect with others in this way then you should not do it. You could simply remember to be mindful when meeting other people and stay present with them. An inauthentic experience of where you are pretending and trying to be interested in what the person is saying can be worse than not talking to them at all.

Living on purpose

Sometimes your purpose in life can transcend all other aspects of presence. People like Mother Theresa, Gandhi and Mandela did not always dress in a powerful way, did not stand in a powerful way but nonetheless, each through having the confidence of their purpose, were able to speak in a way that invoked presence. People who came into contact with them felt this presence and energy in their interactions with them. When you become congruent with your purpose in life and live and act from this place, you develop a presence that transcends all else about you as the clarity of who and what you are here to do in life, communicates in such a clear and inspiring way.

Why is it important to have presence as a leader?

A leader has a number of influential roles. One of the most high profile roles is as the representative of your organisation as others identify you then directly with the organisation. This may not always be fair or correct but it is important to remember as there are now fewer and fewer boundaries between your roles in life. When representing the organisation in a more formal sense, it is clear that certain behaviours and actions are expected as these directly reflect on the organisation itself. So at industry events, staff parties or conferences, the types of behaviours and activities become much more dictated by the fact that you are there in that role and not as a private citizen.

With the increasing use of social media and technologies there is less differentiation between who you are at work and who you are outside of work. The images and activities that you place in your social media pages now reflect who you are as a whole person, no matter the place, time or situation. People still understand that many aspects revealed on these social platforms are in your private life but still reflect on your image as a leader. They therefore need to be managed as such and inappropriate or damaging imagery and information needs to be removed as soon as possible.

Another area where you are representing your organisation is when you are networking, whether this is with a new client, to your industry peers or to the media. The manner in which you conduct yourself (grooming, voice, and stance) will influence the degree to which you are believed and respected and that you are able to win new clients and partners for the business.

Sylvia Hewlett, CEO of The Center for Talent Innovation, in her book *"Executive Presence"* documents the results of a research study of senior executives which found that executive presence is the key to corporate advancement. Hewlett noted "No man or woman attains a top job, lands an extraordinary deal, or develops a significant following without this heady combination of confidence, poise and authenticity that convinces the rest of us that we're in the presence of someone who's going places. Just witness how far executive presence has propelled the careers of Barack Obama, Christine Lagarde, Steve Jobs, Angela Merkel and Angelina Jolie."[18]

Brand Me

In looking at the different elements in being mindful about your presence as a Leader it is useful to remember that in the end you may need to let go of everything else and really focus on your purpose in life, and to let this ultimately determine what your brand or your image is for you. Choosing to authentically represent the best and clearest presence of who you are will exude the strongest presence. It may not be about how many likes or friends you have on social media because at the end of the day, there are no substitutes for authenticity and being congruent with who you are and what you stand for in the world.

Interview: *The Focused Leader*

Dan founded Forex Nation, the world's 1st charity foreign exchange broker, after leaving a lucrative trading role and in response to a gap she saw in the financial services market. This market had traditionally shared its wealth through some form of community engagement but in being highly conservative defined success in terms of shareholder returns. She had the belief that shareholder returns were no longer the most relevant definition of success; that bigger wasn't better and that the GFC had highlighted consumer dissatisfaction with the excesses of the big end of town.

Dan believes that the old way of corporate thinking "trains people to be unaware so that at the end of the day, at the end of the week, they set themselves up by their own definitions of success to feel bad. That the sole focus on money misses the richness in the moments in life as there is no end goal." The business model for Forex Nation was also set up differently from other players in the financial markets. The standard model is one where market-making brokers make money off traders and investors losing money and so have a vested interest in keeping traders in the dark about industry practices. The Forex Nation difference revolves around voluntary transparency, community and charity.

At the time of interviewing Dan, Forex Nation's trading licence was being renegotiated and the licence partner was requesting 40% of the turnover to renew the licence. To renew the licence would mean that 40% of the money that was generated was not going to charity but to the licence partner. But to not renew the licence would mean that the organisation could not continue to trade with new clients or grow for a period of time.

Faced with this decision she noted that "you get what you focus

CHAPTER 9: PRESENCE IS BEING DRESSED FROM WITHIN

on". Dan was focused on creating an organisation that had trust and a community of leaders that supported what was being built. So instead of choosing to focus on the problems that this might create, she focused on the opportunities of showing the investors and the community what she was building, that this was their current situation and that the licencing would be sorted out with further negotiations with other suppliers. The focus on the new business model with the charity focus meant that traditional financial market business models and deals were no longer appropriate for her organisation.

By showing the vulnerability of the organisation at that time and being mindful of the positives and negatives that were associated with it, Dan's leadership style was reflecting that the "only thing here to do is lead by example mindfully on a moment by moment basis". In creating not only a new 'win-win' business model that redefines how everyone in a financial relationship can succeed, Dan is a guiding light in how mindfulness, even in the moment to moment world of financial market fluctuations, can transform the planet.

~ Danielle Lehrer, Founder Forex Nation, RAC Advisory Board Member

Review: key lessons in the mindful leadership Presence Step

- Presence can be indefinable but it is something that is felt by people around someone who exhibits it
- The Presence Model is made up of a person's image, their confidence, their attitude and the degree to which they are living aligned with their purpose
- Presence is important for a leader. As the representative of the organisation it can determine relationships with staff, clients and other stakeholders
- Social media means that a leader's presence in all areas of their life needs to be managed and maintained

To help integrate what has been covered in this chapter and to begin the journey of understanding Presence more in your life, consider the questions on next page.

Reflective questions

1. Do you think that you have any Presence? Why? Why not?
_____
_____
_____

2. If you wanted to improve your image, confidence or attitude what would you do?
_____
_____
_____

3. Are there things that you can do so that your Presence is more aligned with your Purpose?
___
___
___

4. Have you done a social media audit to see what information and images are out there about you?
___
___
___

5. What sort of Presence do you want to be known for? How are you going to create this?
___
___
___

PART THREE

WHERE TO FROM HERE?

- Conclusion
- Appendix

CONCLUSION

*"Don't worry about what the world needs.
Ask what makes you come alive and do that.
Because what the world needs is people who have come alive."*
~ Howard Thurman

I have never worked in an organisation that wasn't restructuring. As a young adult I used to talk my father about this. His world of work and expectations was very different to the one I had entered into, just as the world of work is now very different to what it was for me when I started. There are, however, some constants that survive these changes, which were there when my father was working and will be there when I have finished working. These are the timeless elements that I have described within the 7 Steps to being a mindful leader.

As human beings we are always trying to understand why we are here. Finding a Purpose for our lives and translating that into a Passion is what adds many layers of richness of experience. As leaders we are constantly making decisions and refining our Pathways to simplify our decision-making processes. We want to be inspirational and move with People we are leading towards a worthwhile vision, creating Prosperity for ourselves and others as we do so. This journey is enhanced by Pausing to renew ourselves with moments of mindfulness.

All these elements then combine into what we put forward through our Presence as the 'brand me' of our leadership style. These are the same human elements that philosophers and poets throughout the history of mankind have been discussing and debating in their own ways.

In researching and writing these 7 Steps I have thought of philosophers often as I focused on different concepts and ideas in each of them. As I grew more mindful of each of the 7 Steps themselves many of them seemed to come alive as I became absorbed in the academic researchers, industry leaders and reading of each area. I wondered how Aristotle, Socrates and Descartes felt as they were writing. Aristotle himself found that ethics were founded on the concept of doing good rather than merely being a good person. I wondered how he came to that conclusion. Did Aristotle research, do interviews with leading people of his age and look back on his experiences over time? Was there an element of the red car syndrome when he was writing?

Just as when you buy a red car, suddenly all you see are red cars around you, when writing about mindful leadership examples of mindful leadership appeared all around me. It was truly amazing how many 'red cars' came forward for me. One of the funniest was when my phone battery died just as I was talking to an editor about how important it is to be mindful in each moment. How embarrassed was I at having ignored the warning beeps!

Another great influence on these writings has been my enjoyment of the science fiction genre over many years. As a Star Trek fan I am sure that I have been subtly brainwashed about the power of structure (Mr Spock) and intuition (Captain Kirk) working together. Mr Spock is the epitome of logic and reasoning and comes to his decisions through a process of deductive reasoning and Captain Kirk seemingly appears to make his decisions solely through what seems to be a good idea at the time. Yet it is through the partnership of these two characters in which each complements the other's strengths which then makes each of them individually expand into being more aware (mindful) of what they do.

CHAPTER 10: CONCLUSION

As organisations struggle to retain good staff, keep up with technology and make decisions about how to grow the organisation could it be as simple as asking what Kirk would do. Or what Spock would do. Or how do I come up with a strategy by being more mindful to myself, other people and other dynamics present in these situations? It follows then that the more mindful you are the more likely you are to make more effective and successful choices.

For example, the more authentic you are in hiring, firing or retaining the right staff for the organisation, the more connected you will be to your staff and your staff to you. People are looking to work for organisations that provide meaning to them and the way to truly develop and show that meaning is by being mindfully authentic.

In managing technology and other operational decisions the challenges are compounded by the variety and amount of information that is required even to have a basic understanding of the area. How much clearer would this information be if when looking at complex information it was the only thing being focused upon?

Mindfulness in the moment assists with focusing only on what you need to know and understand in that moment and leaves everything else aside. Similarly we can apply this approach to growing the organisation. Focusing on each of the strategic choices available so that it is held in its own individual moment would allow greater insights and the embracing of both the information available and your own intuition.

A leader's role is to also lead the management of major compliance risks facing the organisation. How much easier would this be if you were able to apply the 7 Steps of being a mindful leader to each of these types of risks? How would understanding how decisions are made by staff in the organisation assist you in this risk management? Would an authentic conversation with a colleague generate greater clarity about risks than any report into these risks?

It can take a lot of energy to be a leader with meetings, emails, calls coming in a continuous 24/7 stream. So energy management is critical to you and your team to be able to maintain your performance. In mindfully going through each of your time management areas you are able to focus on what you need to be doing and not necessarily what your diary says. By applying these 7 Steps and in particular Pausing, more clarity and focus can be placed on the next steps that will most efficiently and effectively use your time.

After many years of continuous restructuring there are also many change-fatigued people out there who need some form of Pausing within the organisation to assist them with recharging and rebooting who they are in the workplace. Your role is to become a master of an authentic form of Pausing for yourself and then to lead the organisation to determine what structures for Pausing best suits your organisation.

The ongoing applications of mindful leadership are endless and are as varied as people are. As a mindful leader leading strategic planning sessions, product launch events, football practice or the family outing, whatever the situation or circumstance may be, the continuous practice of the 7 Steps to being a mindful leader will assist in achieving those tasks and activities in a more mindful way.

CHAPTER 10: CONCLUSION

So in this moment, what next?

The final section of this book provides some selected exercises for integrating the 7 Steps to being a mindful leader. After the exercises there is further information available about how to participate in more exercises, workshops and programs as a mindful leader. Training, learning and studying about being a mindful leader continues on for the rest of your life. The analogy is that your life is like your car. If you don't maintain it then it either falls apart or you get a bigger bill when you do go to fix it than if you had kept maintaining it along the way. If you don't maintain your mental, physical, emotional and spiritual aspects by being mindfully aware of them, that you too will either fall apart or suffer bigger health, relationship or emotional bills later on.

A final influence worth noting in these writings is the scientific spiritual observer that has walked with me as the words have formed on the pages. I woke many days to write with the intention of sharing my soul song in the words that I would create. I had no structure to follow for how this would manifest but as the structures of the chapters and sections would unfold, so too intuitive elements of the soul song would emerge. When I have felt stuck I would read poetry of someone like Hafiz for inspiration, practice songs I am learning to sing or pause a moment to watch a cloud float by. Activities to consciously focus my mind back into the essence of what I was writing as opposed to the physical word that was being written.

There is a profound saying that 'the Universe rewards action, not thought". What this means is that in the taking the actions to change your life from living in the have-do-be life to the be-do-have approach to life, you are supported to become more of yourself and to live more authentically and on purpose. But that it takes action, actually putting yourself on the line and moving forward. Mindful thought and training alone is insufficient without then taking mindful steps. Einstein said "A person who never made a mistake never tried anything new."[19]

So try something new. Incorporate these 7 Steps into your life. The key in life is to keep growing, to keep moving on, and connecting in more ways to who you are as the great mystery of your life. To connect with others to hear and understand who they are in the mysteries of their lives as well. To connect with communities to hear and understand what your planet, your tribes are also telling you about their great mysteries. By connecting in this way you are living and breathing mindfully your life, your purpose, for your time here in this lifetime.

Go, Be Mindful!

Thank you to the reader...

*"When once a chairperson of a multinational company
came to see me, to offer me a property in Bombay,
he first asked:
'Mother, how do you manage your budget?"
I asked him who had sent him here.
He replied: 'I felt an urge inside me.'
I said:
"Other people like you come to see me and say the same.
It was clear God sent you, Mr. A, as He sends Mr. X, Mrs. Y, Miss Z,
and they provide the material means we need for our work.
The grace of God is what moved you.
You are my budget.
God sees to our needs, as Jesus promised.
I accepted the property he gave and named it
Asha Dan (Gift of Hope)"*

~ Mother Teresa

Blessings to each of you who have read this book. May you continue to be the inspiring mindful leaders that you are and follow your own urges wherever they may take you in your life.

APPENDIX

Selected exercises for integrating the 7 steps to transforming your business and your life.

The selected exercises which follow will continue to train you to be a detached observer of your life so that you can use mindfulness to take control of it.
As a detached observer you become more aware of your thoughts, feelings and emotions without letting yourself be run by them. As a mindful leader you can use this detachment to pause and become aware of what is going on and what the structured or intuitive response options may be for you in that moment.

Exercise 1:
Creating your bucket list

A commonly-used and powerful exercise used to determine your life purpose is writing your own eulogy. Doing this exercise prompts you to look back over your life and to reflect on what you were most proud of and want to be remembered by. By identifying what you want to be remembered for, you can then discover what you want to do in your life. Another way to think of this exercise is to think of what your 'bucket list' would be.

This same exercise can be adapted for when you are leading, or about to lead, an organisation through a transformation. It is a useful exercise as at the end of the transformation, as at the end of life, how you want to be remembered has a profound impact on your motivation to succeed in what you do.

Step 1. Find pen and paper and a quiet place where you will not be disturbed for a while. Some people find being in nature or in one of their favourite spots helps them to unwind and move into a quieter space. This exercise does not work as well with electronic devices, it has to be done with pen and paper.

Step 2. Close your eyes. Count very slowly down from 10 to 1.

Step 3. Open your eyes and ask whatever higher power you believe in to work with you now. If you don't have a higher power then think of a loved one and ask for them to come into your mind to work with you now.

Step 4. Start to write your eulogy. Do not go back and keep reading and re-reading it but just let your thoughts flow and write them down. Write like this for 15 minutes. If you get stuck some questions to ask yourself might be:

What type of person was I?

What did I achieve?

Did I follow my dreams?

Who did I help?

Did I help others follow their dreams?

Did I do what I said I would do?

Did I do what I wanted to do in life?

Did I have a bucket list that I was working through?

Was I respected and loved by others?

Example of a Eulogy:

Minister:

Fred was a loving 80 year old man who will be missed by his children and grandchildren. His wife Suzy has described him as a kind and determined man who supported his family through life's journey. They met and married and raised their family in x and have been active and respected members of their community.

His daughter:

Dad was a loving father who although he was always busy would make time for us kids when we needed him. He loved to play with his grandchildren and was a favourite with them all when he made them balloon animals.

His son:

Dad was an inspiration to me in all I did in my life. His integrity and inclusiveness in how he dealt with people stood out for me when I saw him with people. I remember one time he stopped and started talking to the building cleaner on his way into the office. They talked about the football and I could see how much it meant to the cleaner to be noticed when dad stopped and talked to him. Dad was such a busy and important man who always made people his priority and 'walked the talk' for us kids.

Minister:

Fred was a member of xyz whose mission to save children from the slave trade was a real passion. Under his leadership they were able to influence the governments of many countries to ban all activities which were supporting the slave trade.

He was also a successful businessman who followed his dreams of leading xyz organisation which grew to be a global success under his leadership. He was well known and respected by his peers who found him an inspirational and thoughtful man.

But perhaps what most people remember Fred for is his love of adventure. When Fred achieved each of his dreams, like sailing a boat around the world, walking the Inca trail, or playing golf in St Andrews, he was like a new man and had a new lease on life.

Sadly we will all miss Fred but take comfort that he is at peace now.

APPENDIX: SELECTED EXERCISES

Once you have written your eulogy read it over a few times and as you are reading it ask yourself, what is my life's purpose? Keep reading and asking yourself this question. Write down 3-5 key words that come up as you are asking the question.

Go back and look at the key words and write them into a sentence which starts:

My bucket list is...................

☙❧☙❧☙❧☙❧

Exercise 2:
Connect to your life purpose

This is one of the most simple and profound ways to connect inwardly and to quieten the outer world long enough to start to hear the inner world. To start find a quiet spot and turn off any devices. Place a blank piece of paper and a pen in front of you. This doesn't work with laptops etc. It has to be a pen and paper.

Allocate 15 minutes to finding your life purpose (trust me - you are worth spending 15 minutes on this!!)

Step 1. Try to stop breathing. Test this out 2-3 times.

Step 2. Notice what happens when you try to stop breathing. You reached a point where you have to start breathing again. Your body takes over and starts to breathe you again. Is that you breathing? Are you choosing to breathe at that point? What part of you is it that has taken that gulp of air when you tried to stop breathing? Start to notice how busy your mind is.

Step 3. Now try to slow down your breathing. Breathe in and breathe out to the count of 5 each way. Inhale, two three four five. Exhale, two three, four five. Do this 10 times and notice as you are doing it how your body starts to relax. Your mind is still there but it is less busy, and focusing on your breath and counting is slowing everything down.

Step 4. Now count backwards from 10 down to 1 counting out each of the numbers as you do on an outbreath. 10 (breath out), breath in, 9 (breath out), breath in.... do this slowly and as you are breathing in and out take about 6 seconds for each way. Notice that your mind is even calmer now.

Step 5. Continue breathing as in Step 4. Now as you finish each round and get to 1 ask yourself, what is my life's purpose? As you ask yourself this question write whatever comes to mind on the paper in front of you. Continue on and do this five times. Each time write what comes to mind on the piece of paper. Do not read what you have written but stay focused on the breathing. Let your thoughts just flow and whatever comes out be okay.

Step 6. To finish, just sit quietly and close your eyes. Thank yourself for placing you as being important in your life and for taking the time to do this exercise. The information that you have gained about your life purpose is a gift to yourself and you are very grateful for it.

Step 7. Now read and re-read what you have written and as you are reading it ask yourself, what is my life's purpose? Look for words that are repeated or phrases that came up a few times. Summarise it down into 3-5 points that resonate as your life's purpose for you.

Go back and look at the key words, choose 3 of them, write them into a sentence which starts:

My life purpose is...................

Try to schedule a quiet period after doing an exercise like this but if you are not able to then just be as gentle with yourself as you can.

Exercise 3:
Sleeping with your conscience at night

As a mindful leader I, like many others, have had to face serious difficulties where the question of sleeping with my conscience has been foremost in my mind. At these challenging points in time I wished that I had some clear steps like below to help me navigate my way through the challenges. May these now help you:

Step 1: Write down what you would or would not feel like doing about this situation

Step 2: Write down the best and the worst thing that could happen to you

Step 3: Write down the best and the worst thing that could happen to others

Step 4: Think about this as if it was on the front page of the newspaper. Have I covered my actions/ inactions sufficiently?

Step 5: Think about what people 100 years from now would say about your actions or inactions

Step 6: Draw a line down the middle of a blank piece of paper. On one side (A) of the line write the reasons for doing something and on the other side (B) write the reasons for not doing something.

Step 7: Set up three chairs: A, B and C. Chair A is you the person with the reasons for doing something and chair B is you the person with the reasons for not doing something

Step 8: Go and sit in Chair A and read the list A (for doing something) out loud. Notice how you feel and what reactions come up for you as you read the list aloud

Step 9: Go and sit in chair B and read the list B (for not doing something) out loud. Notice how you feel and what reactions come up for you as you read the list aloud

Step 10: Go and sit on chair C and look back chairs A and B. You will now have an answer as to what you feel you should do. Again notice what your mind is doing with this information. Just notice it and see what is coming up for you

Step 11: While still sitting in chair C agree within yourself about your decision and also agree within yourself that you will be able to handle the consequences of the decision, although unknown at that point in time, as you have all the skills and experience to do so.

Step 12: Get up and go and implement your decision.

Exercise 4:
Clearing out your head (mind clearing)

Step 1: Get a clean piece of paper and just begin to write everything that comes to mind. It must be with pen and paper to allow your mind to just free form with whatever is present in it. The process does not work as well with electronic devices.

Step 2: Write for at least 10 minutes until you have listed everything that you can think of.

Step 3: Organise your thoughts. Now look back at what you have written and start to organise it. This can now be done electronically using mind mapping or even in a simple chart format like below. The titles of each of the columns should be ones that suit what you have written and reflect what is then written under it.

Step 4: Some of what you have written is for things that may take longer to achieve. For those items write them under a heading such as "Projects" or "5 year plan".

This is different from the things that you wrote under the 'someday/maybe' column. The things in this column reflect more of a wish list of things that you would like to do someday as at this point in time. This column changes as things become more or less important over the years and those things that stay in this column over time also reflect what it is you really want to do.

The things that stay in this column consistently over a period of years would go into your 'bucket list' that you have for your life and be prioritised in your 5 year plan to do at some point.

Step 5: Now allocate dates and perhaps specific times to when you will complete the activities. Some of them may be grouped

APPENDIX: SELECTED EXERCISES

like 1 hour for phone calls on 5th October. There are many time management applications available now which can be loaded to any personal device so one of these could now be used to manage the tasks on this list.

Date	Calls	Email	Shops/ When Out	To Do	Projects	5 year plan	Someday/ Maybe
e.g. 5th Oct at 5pm for 1 hr	e.g. Keith, Maree, Andrew						

ଏହା

Exercise 5:
Weird synchronicities that work

It is an unusual occurrence, but one that has been observed many times, that the opening of a random book at a random page can seem to contain a direct message for the situation you are working with at the time. The exercise below looks at this more closely.

Step 1: Pick up any book or brochure around you and open it randomly to a page.

Step 2: Pick a paragraph on the page of that book and write it out on a separate page.

Step 3: Look at the separate page and reflect on the following questions:

Did you agree or disagree with what is stated in the paragraph?
Did you trust or not trust what is stated in the paragraph?
How did the paragraph leave you feeling after you wrote it down? (happy, sad, elated, deflated?)

Step 4: Write your answers to the questions in 3 that you have been thinking about underneath the paragraph.

Step 5: Review the paragraph from the book, review what you wrote about the paragraph, and notice how it all makes you feel, what you are thinking, and whether or not you are inspired to action.

Step 6: Now reflect on the whole exercise ~ picking a random paragraph, reviewing the paragraph from the perspective of your moral compass (agree/disagree etc.) and what you have learnt about yourself.

This exercise can be repeated at any time with any book or information.

APPENDIX: SELECTED EXERCISES

Exercise 6: Get creative about what you want to do (mind mapping)

To do a mind map take a blank piece of paper and write the word with your main thought in the centre of it. Next to this main thought write other words that relate to this thought and draw circles around them. Add any notes, comments, and ideas to these circles or 'thought bubbles' as well.

Soon you will have a whole lot of information around the main thought that you have developed and you will have other flows of ideas and information that seem to flow out from this thought.

Now you have a visual map of this information you can then start to plan using something like the table in the mind clearing (exercise 5) to decide how and what you are going to do and prioritise next.

As in time management, there are many applications for mind mapping that can also be used in this process. It is good to experiment with doing this on paper and then electronically and to use whichever works best for you.

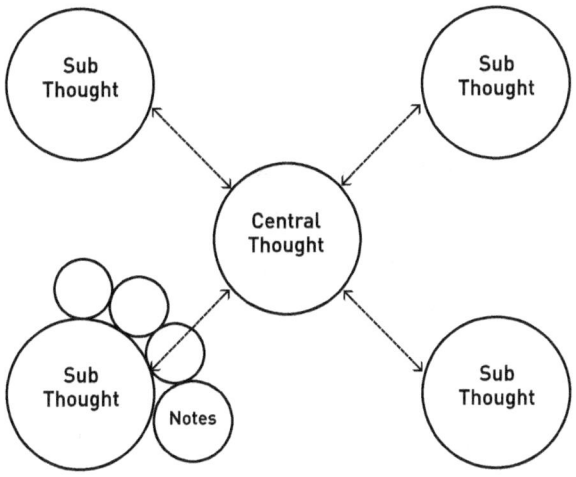

Exercise 7: The world is your stage (retrain the mind by acting as if...)

Once you have a better understanding of what is on your mind (exercise 4 - mind clearing) and where those thoughts are leading you (exercise 6 - mind mapping), the next exercise is to start to program some positive ways in which to focus your thoughts so that you can begin to act as if these thoughts were already true.

I AM.... Accepting myself
Accepting others
Alive
Allowing myself the dignity of my own expression
Attracting good experiences in life to me
Attracting good people to me
Attracting good things to me
Balanced
Beautiful
Being compassionate with myself more each day
Being exquisitely gentle with myself
Blessed
Caring
Centred inside myself
Choosing how to live my life
Compassionate
Compassionate to myself
Compassionate to others
Courageous
Embracing all parts of myself and loving them all

I AM.... Embracing change in my life
Embracing each moment of my life fully
Enjoying the journey of my life
Feeling the support of others in my life
Forgiving myself
Forgiving others
Free
Full of knowing
Full of wisdom
Fun
Funny
Gorgeous
Gifted
Giving
Giving myself the freedom to feel alive
Giving myself the gift of enjoying my life
Giving myself the gift of time out from my normal day
Giving myself the space in my life to just spend time with me
Giving myself the time to plan my life that I need
Giving myself the time to rest that I need
Giving praise when praise is due to myself
Grateful
Grateful for everything in my life
Grateful for my family
Grateful for my friends
Grateful for my lifestyle

I AM.... Grateful for the opportunities in my life
Grateful for the people in my life
Growing each day in loving myself more
Growing each day in understanding myself
Happy
Healthy
Humble
Humbled by the gifts given to me in my life
Inspired
Joyful
Kind to myself
Kind to others
Learning to be more relaxed about my future
Learning to be present to each moment of my life
Learning to let go of the past
Listening fully to myself
Listening fully to others
Living a rich lifestyle
Living abundantly
Living easily
Living gracefully
Living the best I know how in this moment now
Loving
Loving myself more each day
Open to change in my life
Open to hearing my own inner voice
Open to new possibilities and ideas in my life

APPENDIX: SELECTED EXERCISES

I AM....
- Open to new ideas
- Open to receiving
- Organised
- Pausing when I feel busy and taking time out for myself
- Peaceful
- Precious
- Present in this moment
- Present to the precious gift of now
- Relaxed
- Speaking kind words to myself
- Speaking kind words to others
- Supporting myself in my life
- Supporting the planet in my caring actions
- Taking care of myself in a loving and gentle way
- Talented
- Trusting myself
- Trusting that everything happens for a reason
- Trusting that everything will be okay
- Trusting that I am guided perfectly through life
- Trusting that I can manage everything that comes to me in life
- Understanding myself each day more and more
- Willing to let go of the past
- Willing to step into my future
- Wise
- Wonderful
- Worthy

Exercise 8:
Using a repetitive speech technique

People can go into fear and strong reactions when faced with change. What they are looking for is reassurance that there is a reason for the change and by using a repetitive speech technique, like a broken record that goes over and over the same spot, you can reinforce the vision of what the change is trying to do to and provide the reassurance that they are looking for. This can be a powerful tool for reinforcing a message.

In repeating the message (e.g. the vision for the future after the change) over and over as to why the organisation is going through this change it can help to break through the anxiety that people are experiencing with the change. This is not to discount what is being said about the problems or issues, but to reinforce that there is a valid reason as to why the discomfort is being felt.

The other side of this is also that if people understand the bigger "why" (the vision) of what is happening to them they will accept it faster and more readily, even if they do not agree with it.

This repetition speech technique can be used to not only convince others but also yourself of key messages that you may want to reinforce, in a similar way that affirmations are used.

Exercise 9:
Two sides to every coin
(people's reactions to change)

Ask the person to draw a line dividing a blank piece of paper and on one side write the benefits and on the other side of the line, the drawbacks of what is happening to them in the change.

Step 1: Set up three chairs. Chair A represents for the person the benefits of what is happening and chair B represents for the person the drawbacks of what is happening

Step 2: Ask the person to now go and sit in chair A and to read the list of benefits of what is happening to them out loud. Ask them to notice how they feel and what reactions come up for them as they read the list aloud

Step 3: Ask the person to now go and sit in the chair B and read the list of drawbacks of what is happening to them out loud

Step 4: Now ask them to go and sit in chair C and look back at chairs A and B. Ask them to notice what their mind is doing with this information. They should just observe and remain detached to just be present with what is coming up for them

Step 5: Discuss with the person if they can see both benefits and drawbacks of what is happening to them with the changes

It is normal for a lot of resistance to the exercise itself to emerge as there are a lot of charged emotions with the change itself. The suggestion is that the technique be shown to staff and then they are asked to practise it a few times as each time they go through the process there will be more clarity into the process and options for them.

Exercise 10:
Let the pen take you where it wants to go (free form writing)

Writing to connect to what you are thinking and how you are feeling can be one of the most helpful tools to determine what you do and don't want out of situations. The technique of free-form writing is where you write and write and do not stop. It is important to not read what you are writing and at the end of writing to dispose of what you have written either by burning, shredding or flushing it down the toilet.

It may seem a bit counter-intuitive at first to be writing and then to throw it away but think of the mind being like a dirty glass that has been stirred up and the writing process a way of filling the glass with water to get all the dirt out of it. Would you then want to drink the dirty water? No, you wouldn't. The clarity comes from clearing the mind (rinsing the glass) and once that dirt is gone being able to see more clearly what it is you want to get out of the situation.

This is a very powerful tool and should not be done for more than 10 minutes at a time.

APPENDIX: SELECTED EXERCISES

Exercise 11:
Gratitude journaling

Another writing method is to begin a gratitude journal where each day you record what you are grateful for giving and grateful for receiving. This journal can be the container of all the ideas, activities and items that you place out in the world that you would like to receive and also what you would like to give.

The act of writing things down is a very powerful one and can help to clarify what you are focusing on in ways that can begin to make it much more real.

☙❧❧❧❧

Exercise 12:
A love letter to yourself

Another very powerful writing technique is where you write a love letter to yourself. In writing the letter think of yourself as your greatest supporter, your biggest fan. As someone who wants the best for you and wants you to succeed in everything that you do. Find a quiet time and place to write the letter and have a stamped envelope ready with you to seal it at the end.

It may help to imagine yourself as a young child that you are writing to. What words of caring and loving would you write to that young child? How much enthusiasm would you share for how successful the child has been in their life to date?

Let your imagination and playful side come out as you write the precious words to the most important person in the world ~ you.

Exercise 13:
For everything there is a season meditation

Read this meditation onto a recorder with your own voice and then play it back to yourself. If some words don't fit for you then change them so that they are words that you would use.

The purpose of this meditation is to connect to the whole circle of life ~ beginning, middle and end ~ by consciously connecting to your own sense that each part is natural, a part of the whole transformation process called life, and that it is supported.

Start:

In an old old forest many miles from here stands a big wise old gum tree. The tree has been alive for as long as anyone can remember and marks the passing of time for all who live there. For some it had been as tall as their house when they used to play under it, for others as tall as the town church, and for the youngest, it had always seemed to reach up touching the sky. You have had a calling all of your life to visit this magnificent gum tree and now it is time for you to go.

You can imagine yourself now walking down a long winding path, passing through the highlights of your life. As you go, start to observe what it is that has brought you to who you are now. Just acknowledge these events, these markers and then let them go as you continue to walk down this path. The path has many twists and turns, highs and lows. Maintain a deep sense of compassion for yourself. See each change in the path and know that you did the best you could at the time. Let all your judgements go as you continue walking down this path.

Let emotions come up but remain the observer to them all and just let them wash through you as you breathe in and breathe out. Keep breathing deeply and if it starts to feel too much focus more on your breath to bring you back to centre so that you can continue walking down your path.

Your path now leads you past a junkyard. You can't quite make out what is there but you get a sense that it is full of a lot of junk, uncompleted projects, some incompletions from your life. Just observe again and don't try to work out what is there just be present to your experience of passing this on your path. Acknowledge that it is there for now.

Continue walking until you come to the end of the path and in a clearing you see the old old gum tree. The tree invites you to go over and sit under it and to rest for a while. Just sit there with this timeless tree. You do not need to do anything. Just observe the tree, your surroundings, the smells, the sights, the sounds. Just spend a moment connecting with your surroundings as you sit under the tree. Do not do anything, just become present to the tree. Let go of the journey, the path that brought you here and connect to you. Immerse yourself in the stillness of just being you, of just sitting there under the tree. You don't need to do, say, have anything, you can just be. Just stay with that for a few minutes.

In this stillness a flower falls from the sky onto the ground in front of you. Just look at the flower. It is old and brown and wrinkled. It has so many signs on it of a very long life. You notice the colours, the textures, the smells and the sounds around you as it falls to the ground. Just observe the flower. Acknowledge that this is the end of its life and that as it let go of the tree it knew that it was the end. Imagine yourself as this flower, letting go of, of surrendering to, the end.

APPENDIX: SELECTED EXERCISES

As you sit there observing the flower, time seems to speed up, the flower begins to decompose, your vision gets blurry, you hear many different sounds, smell different smells and feel different sensations, and then this whirlwind of time passes and all is still again.

You look out clearly again and where there was the decomposing flower is a young gum tree. It is a miracle. A seed in the old flower had used the decomposing old flower as food to fuel its growth and is now there is a strong young tree playing with the wind. As you watch you see more leaves and flowers growing on this new tree. Each of them hearing the stories of their ancestor that surrendered his life so that they may have theirs. A story that had been told by flowers to their children through time immemorial.

You sense that it is time for you to leave now and so you thank the young gum tree and the old gum tree for letting you visit and then start back down your path. You feel yourself connecting more and more back into your body as you walk down the path. Your feet on the floor, your body in the chair, the sounds in the room and when you feel ready, gently open your eyes.

Take out some paper and draw or write about your experiences on this journey. Imagine yourself as the old flower, the decomposing flower and then the new gum tree. Which part of you is the old old gum tree? How has this story helped you to connect to some parts of you that have maybe died to help other parts of you live throughout your life? What are some experiences that may have felt like the decomposing flower in your life? Write about anything else that has come to mind.

Exercise 14: Be the best you that you can be (Presence Checklist)

The Presence Model Area	Checklist	Ways to Improve them
Image	e.g. Teeth Hair Makeup/ Face Hair Clothes Shoes Nails Blemishes Handbag/ Bag Phone Jewellery Underwear	e.g. whitening
Confidence	Body posture Voice projection Speech clarity Ability to instruct others	
Attitude	Positive attitudes Negative attitudes Ability to listen Interest in Others Able to keep eye contact Able to tell someone that they are a valued person Able to give constructive criticism	

The Presence Model Area	Checklist	Ways to Improve them
Living on Purpose	Living my life in alignment with my purpose	
	Clear about who I am	
	Clear about what I am doing in my life	
	Can clearly explain what my purpose is to others	

Exercise 15:
Celebrating the gift called Life

Parents place the drawings and other loving mementos from their kids on the fridge and other places where everyone in the family can see them. Organisations have the employee of the month on noticeboards so that everyone in the organisation can see them. So where is the wall where all of your successes every day, every year are kept? You don't have one? So it is time to build one!

Find a place in your home that is just your spot. It may be a part of a wall, a notice board, etc. it isn't important what it is, what is important is that everyone else in your home knows that this is your space, and only yours. They can also be encouraged to create their own space for themselves as well if they want to. Decide how you are going to decorate this space and show its boundaries. Some people with enough space create man caves or women caves. If you have a large space such as this then still pick a wall or a particular place which is just for your successes that you are grateful for.

Then each day visit this place and write at least one thing that you were grateful and successful in your life on that day. Even on the days when nothing seemed to go right – the kids got thrown out of school, you lost your job, the car broke down – write one thing that you can celebrate for that day, e.g. with no job I get to spend more time with my kids.

After a few days, a few weeks, you will start to see how you truly are a winner every day of every year in your life.

Bibliography

1. Dominic White, *"Mindfulness: modern management of stress"*. The Australian Financial Review, 1 September 2014.
2. William A. Gentry, Regina H. Eckert, Sarah A. Stawiski and Sophia Zhao. *"The Challenges Leaders Face Around the World: More Similar than Different"* (2014), Centre for Creative Leadership.
3. Roy F. Baumeister and Kathleen D. Vohs. *"The pursuit of meaningfulness in life."* Handbook of Positive Psychology (2002), page 613.
4. Roy F. Baumeister and Kathleen D. Vohs. *"The pursuit of meaningfulness in life."* Handbook of Positive Psychology (2002) page 610.
5. Abridged from Steve Jobs interview with Betsy Morris, Fortune (March 2008)
6. Ethics Resource Center National Ethics Survey (2009) online reporting, http://www.ethicsworld.org/ethicsandemployees/nbes.php
7. Louis Fischer, *"Mahatma Gandhi - His Life and Times"*, Bharatiya Vidya Bhavan publishers (1951)
8. Claudia Dreifus, *"Through Analysis, Gut Reaction Gains Credibility"*. nytimes.com, 28 August, 2007
9. Harold Carey, *"Trust your gut, value your intuition"*. Elearning101.org, 10 November 2007
10. Katherine Hyatt, *"The Influence of Vision on Perceived Organisational Support,"* Kravis Leadership Institute, Leadership Review, vol.11, Spring 2011, page 164
11. Katherine Hyatt, *"The Influence of Vision on Perceived Organisational Support,"* Kravis Leadership Institute, Leadership Review, vol.11, Spring 2011, page 164
12. Erika Andersen, *"11 Quotes from Sir Richard Branson on Business, Leadership, and Passion"*, Forbes, March 2013
13. Amazon, information cited on Wikipedia
14. Arthur C. Brooks, *"Handsome is As Handsome Gives"*, Wall Street Journal, November 2013
15. Arthur C. Brooks, *"Does Giving Make Us Prosperous"*, Journal of Economics and Finance, Volume 31, Number 3, Fall 2007, page 403
16. Lao-Tzu, Tao Te Ching, chapter 64
17. Jon Kabat-Zinn, information cited on Wikipedia
18. Sylvia Hewlett, *Executive Presence: The Missing Link Between Merit and Success*, (2014)
19. Albert Einstein, information cited on Wikipedia

Acknowledgements

There are many dear people, dear souls whom I met through the journey of creating this book and who contributed to it in different ways.

The book elders:

A heartfelt thank you to Sumitra Menon (book editor extraordinaire) who helped to craft poetry from the essence of my ideas, handled grammatical transgressions with humour, and really understood the gift I was creating. It was a joy to work with her.

A heartfelt thank you to James Curtis (branding, book cover and layout) who helped to give visual beauty and elegance to the playground of my ideas, understood the dynamics of structure and intuitive thinking, weaved these throughout and held the vision with me of what we were creating as it unfolded.

A heartfelt thank you to the thought leaders who allowed me to interview them and use that information to present a small part of their stories: Gordon Cairns, Yolanda Vega, Martin Martinez, Lisa Chung, Ruth Medd, Ben Faiz, John Kobal, Neil Thompson and Danielle Lehrer. These truly mindful leaders were a real joy to connect with.

A heartfelt thank you to Andrew Griffiths for practical training in how to go about creating a book and his endorsement and enthusiasm during this journey.

A heartfelt thank you to Danielle Lehrer for writing the foreword and supporting me in many ways, as a fellow change maker in building the vision for a more mindful world.

Thank you to my friends and family: my dearly departed mother and father, Violet and Edwin, sister Linda, brother Malcolm, nieces Kristen, Kaliesha, Evie and Julia, nephews Razali, Omar, Imran, Alexander, Sharif and Nasim, adopted brother Keith Ripper, adopted Hawaiian sister Kathleen Campbell, adopted Chilean sister Francisca Briones, soul sister Caroline Rose, Canadian buddy Sue Chilton, and my dearest friends Victor Taseff, Lena Smarrelli, Lyn Treloar, Diane Hardiman, Andrew Davidson and Maree Lennox.

Thank you to my teachers and guides: J-R, John Morton, Brian Yeakey, Jim Gordon, Robin Ferguson, Nicola Lambert, Rain Czupryna, Shane Hill, Cheryl Alderman, Jen Harwood, John Demartini, Julian Noel and Moose Miller.

Special thanks as well to David Duggan, Glen Carlson, Jane Jackson, Brad Eisenhuth, Robin Powis and Jesper Lowgren. Writing a book is a long and evolving process and I thank these people for their support and feedback. Especially in the early days when I couldn't find the words to explain what I was talking about, they hung in there with me until I nailed it ~ you guys are awesome!

Further Information

Michele Gennoe is a woman on a mission. She is passionate about helping leaders to be more mindful so they can live both meaningful and profitable lives by following the 7 Steps, Purpose, Passion, Pathways, People, Prosperity, Pausing and Presence, to being a Mindful Leader.

Michele's business experience spans 27 years in executive management and senior consulting roles in Australia, Europe and South America. She holds postgraduate qualifications on International Management and a Masters in Spiritual Science. As a natural change maker Michele brings out the best in people and empowers change, often in complex and multi-cultural environments. She has worked in the strategic and organisational change areas on start-up projects in 31 different industry sectors.

With many years in the corporate and personal development worlds Michele is comfortable in both. Her latest book, "Mindful Leadership: 7 steps to transforming your business and your life" is a culmination of her extensive work in these areas and in particular on strategy, organisational change, planning and personal development.

Michele is also an energetic and engaging facilitator. She draws on her own life experiences and compassion to deliver powerful messages in an engaging and authentic way.

Michele consults on strategic planning, organisational change, mindful leadership and personal development.

Put simply Michele provides profound and mindful clarity that empowers leaders and changes the way that they think about their lives.

For further information about workshops, executive coaching and tailored leadership programs or to book a speaking engagement please contact **michele@michelegennoe.com**

Notes

Notes

www.ingramcontent.com/pod-product-compliance
Lightning Source LLC
Chambersburg PA
CBHW070605010526
44118CB00012B/1448